eyes major in the play

THE FOLGER LIBRARY SHAKESPEARE

Designed to make Shakespeare's classic plays available to the general reader, each edition contains a reliable text with modernized spelling and punctuation, scene-by-scene plot summaries, and explanatory notes clarifying obscure and obsolete expressions. An interpretive essay and accounts of Shakespeare's life and theater form an instructive preface to each play.

Louis B. Wright, General Editor, was the Director of the Folger Shakespeare Library from 1948 until his retirement in 1968. He is the author of *Middle-Class Culture in Elizabethan England, Religion and Empire, Shakespeare for Everyman,* and many other books and essays on the history and literature of the Tudor and Stuart periods.

Virginia Lamar, Assistant Editor, served as research assistant to the Director and Executive Secretary of the Folger Shakespeare Library from 1946 until her death in 1968. She is the author of *English Dress in the Age of Shakespeare* and *Travel and Roads in England,* and coeditor of William Strachey's *Historie of Travell into Virginia Britania.*

The Folger Shakespeare Library

The Folger Shakespeare Library in Washington, D.C., a research institute founded and endowed by Henry Clay Folger and administered by the Trustees of Amherst College, contains the world's largest collection of Shakespeareana. Although the Folger Library's primary purpose is to encourage advanced research in history and literature, it has continually exhibited a profound concern in stimulating a popular interest in the Elizabethan period.

A complete brochure of the materials produced under the guidance of Louis B. Wright and Virginia A. LaMar—texts of the plays, supplementary reading, and recordings—is available free on request from Washington Square Press, a Simon & Schuster division of Gulf & Western Corporation, Educational Department, 1230 Avenue of the Americas, New York, N.Y. 10020.

GENERAL EDITOR

LOUIS B. WRIGHT

Director, Folger Shakespeare Library, 1948–1968

ASSISTANT EDITOR

VIRGINIA A. LaMAR

Executive Secretary, Folger Shakespeare Library, 1946–1968

The Folger Library General Reader's Shakespeare

THE TRAGEDY OF MACBETH

by

WILLIAM SHAKESPEARE

WASHINGTON SQUARE PRESS
PUBLISHED BY POCKET BOOKS NEW YORK

A Washington Square Press/Pocket Books Publication
POCKET BOOKS, a Simon & Schuster division of
GULF & WESTERN CORPORATION
1230 Avenue of the Americas, New York, N.Y. 10020

ISBN: 0-671-83550-5

First Pocket Books printing May, 1959

39 38 37 36 35 34 33 32

Printed in the U.S.A.

Preface

This edition of *Macbeth* is designed to make available a readable text of one of Shakespeare's most popular plays. In the centuries since Shakespeare many changes have occurred in the meanings of words, and some clarification of Shakespeare's vocabulary may be helpful. To provide the reader with necessary notes in the most accessible format, we have placed them on the pages facing the text that they explain. We have tried to make these notes as brief and simple as possible. Preliminary to the text we have also included a brief statement of essential information about Shakespeare and his stage. Readers desiring more detailed information should refer to the books suggested in the references, and if still further information is needed, the bibliographies in those books will provide the necessary clues to the literature of the subject.

The early texts of all of Shakespeare's plays provide only inadequate stage directions and it is conventional for modern editors to add many that clarify the action. Such additions, and additions to entrances, are placed in square brackets.

All illustrations are from material in the Folger Library collections.

L. B. W.
V. A. L.

September 1, 1958

A Study in Evil

When Shakespeare wrote *Macbeth,* many of his greatest plays were behind him. From references in the play there is evidence that *Macbeth* dates from about 1606. In chronology it therefore comes between *King Lear* and *Antony and Cleopatra.* The dramatist had already established his reputation in tragedy with *Romeo and Juliet, Julius Cæsar, Hamlet,* and, more recently, *Othello* and *King Lear.* As in *King Lear,* Shakespeare turned to ancient British history for a theme, and chose the career of a Scottish king recounted in Raphael Holinshed's *Chronicles,* that storehouse of plots to which Shakespeare and his contemporaries so often turned. The career of Macbeth is nearer to Shakespeare's age and less vague in date than that of King Lear, for Macbeth was a contemporary of Edward the Confessor, King of England from 1042 to 1066, whose death and vacant throne tempted William of Normandy to cross the Channel. But Shakespeare is less interested in the historical Macbeth than in the Macbeth whom he himself created from hints that he received from Holinshed, a Macbeth whom he studies with the interest of a clinician.

As in all of his great tragedies, Shakespeare is concerned with the study of character, with contrasts in characters, and with motivations. Critics have seen in *Macbeth* a concentration upon the theme of ambition or upon the manifestations of fear with its devastating results. It is perhaps more accurate to say that Shakespeare is here concerned with the corroding effects produced when his protagonist chooses Evil as his good.

A persistent theme in the morality plays and in many later dramas was the struggle between good and evil angels for the soul of man. In the morality plays, the struggle was made explicit, with the good and evil angels as part of the dramatis personae. Even more sophisticated plays, such as Christopher Marlowe's *Doctor Faustus,* might retain this struggle, and in other plays the conflict might be symbolized. In *Macbeth* the struggle for the soul of the chief character is less pronounced, because he falls an easy victim to the promptings of ambition, stimulated by the witches' prophecies; but nevertheless the audience is aware of Macbeth's own debate with his conscience. He tries, however weakly, to put Satan behind him, and it is Lady Macbeth, playing the role of an evil angel, who finally pushes him over the brink into the Bottomless Pit whence there is no return.

Having succumbed to his ambition to gain the Crown by whatever means, Macbeth murders Duncan, a guest in his castle, and this deed inexorably commits him to a career of Evil which leads to ruin. He can never turn back and seek redemption. Once set upon his course, he moves from one act of violence to another in an effort to protect himself from inevitable disaster. Fear and hatred induce him to plot the murder of Banquo and his son, for Banquo cannot help suspecting Macbeth's complicity in Duncan's death, and Banquo's progeny instead of Macbeth's are destined to rule. Enraged at Macduff's failure to support him, he sends assassins to wipe out his family and by this act of cruelty makes certain of Macduff's implacable revenge. In the vain endeavor to insure the security of the throne that he has obtained through violence, he adds evil to evil until he is a byword in Scotland for tyranny and iniquity.

Yet Shakespeare does not make a monster of Macbeth. To have done so would have robbed him of any sympathy and removed him from the area of tragic interest. When the play opens he is a hero returning from the victorious defense of his country. Undoubtedly he has thought about his chances of gaining the throne, for the witches echo things in the dark recesses of his mind, but he shrinks from the violence required to seize the Crown. He is willing to show patience and wait. "If chance will have me King, why, chance may crown me,/ Without my stir." He is near of kin to the King and under the laws of Scotland he may be chosen to succeed Duncan. It is only when Duncan creates his son Malcolm Prince of Cumberland and nominates him as his successor that Macbeth is ripe for murder.

Lady Macbeth is made of sterner stuff than her husband, but she is something more than the cold-blooded virago portrayed by some actresses. Swept away with ambition for her husband's aggrandizement, and with an opportunity suddenly placed before her, she is willing to stifle every good impulse that might keep him "from the golden round," the crown that means the supreme accomplishment of her hopes for him and for herself. In the soliloquy in Act I, Sc.v, she deliberately chooses Evil as her course and invokes the Powers of Darkness to be her aids. Henceforth she will herself be Macbeth's Evil Genius, but she is not mere abstract Evil. She remains a woman, a woman intent upon helping her husband, though that aid may be wicked. She

Lady Macbeth

retains some shreds of human feelings. She might have slain Duncan had he not looked so much like her father. She suffers remorse over her deeds, and that remorse drives her to the self-revelation of the great sleepwalking scene and eventually to her hinted suicide.

Shakespeare is not interested in abstractions but in living human beings and the effects of their deeds upon their characters. In *Macbeth* the author reveals the tragedy that befalls two people who elect to follow a course of evil for the satisfaction of their own ambition. They are people whom the audience will recognize as not beyond their comprehension as living personalities. Though their places may be exalted and their actions beyond those of normal human experience, their feelings and motivations are within the realm of ordinary human understanding, and the spectator can experience the catharsis of pity and fear which comes from identification with the protagonist of a tragedy.

The corrosive effect of Evil upon Macbeth is cumulative until the great scene near the end of the play when he receives news of Lady Macbeth's death. Numb with accumulated horrors, he no longer feels any great emotion, even at the death of the wife who had been his strength, and he merely thinks bitterly that she could have chosen some more convenient time: "She should have died hereafter." For Macbeth the world has turned to ashes and he pours out his disillusionment in one of the great passages of the play:

> Tomorrow, and tomorrow, and tomorrow
> Creeps in this petty pace from day to day
> To the last syllable of recorded time;
> And all our yesterdays have lighted fools

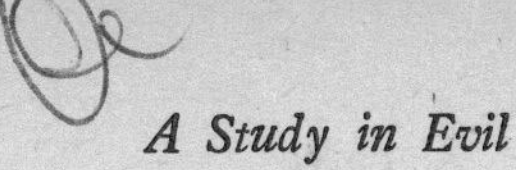

> The way to dusty death. Out, out, brief candle!
> Life's but a walking shadow, a poor player,
> That struts and frets his hour upon the stage
> And then is heard no more. It is a tale
> Told by an idiot, full of sound and fury,
> Signifying nothing.

In *Macbeth* Shakespeare shows more than usual care to fit the atmosphere to the mood and action of the play. Although the authenticity of some of the witch scenes has been questioned, Shakespeare undoubtedly intended that the opening scene and others where the witches appear should set the tone of impending Evil and should suggest the dark thoughts in Macbeth's mind and the dark deeds to follow. Critics have not all agreed about the nature of the witches. Because Holinshed called them the Weird Sisters—the classical Fates or the Norns of Norse mythology—some have thought that Shakespeare simply took over the notion of the goddesses of destiny, who determined man's fate beforehand, in order to emphasize the fatalistic qualities of *Macbeth*. According to this view, he had to make these goddesses understandable in a Scottish play by giving them the attributes of witches, which were familiar to his audience. Perhaps Shakespeare himself was not altogether certain as to the precise qualities of his witches, for he was not a professor of comparative folklore but a highly competent dramatist who understood the effectiveness of witch scenes in providing stage atmosphere. These scenes were even more effective in Shakespeare's time than in ours because most spectators then believed implicitly in witchcraft.

The tension of the play is increased by the frequent

A Renaissance conception of the classical Fates.

From Vincenzo Cartari, *Imagini delli dei de gl'antichi* (1587).

use of dramatic irony. When Duncan heaps praises and honors upon Macbeth, the audience already knows that Macbeth is revolving in his mind the murder of the King. When Duncan talks of the pleasant and peaceful atmosphere of Macbeth's castle and Banquo refers to the swallows that have chosen his castle walls because of their safety and peace, the spectators know that the castle will soon be a house of death.

Macbeth is a dramatic poem with subtleties that only a great poet could have achieved, but it is also a skillfully written stage piece composed by a man who knew the requirements of the theatre. In any analysis of the characters and study of the structure of the play, one should always remember that Shakespeare is first and last a man of the theatre and is writing for theatrical interpretation. His was never the art of the closet dramatist, and he did not belabor his Muse to inspire mysteries that only the diligent scholar under his midnight lamp could unravel. *Macbeth* is one of the best illustrations of Shakespeare's competence as a writer for the public stage.

TEXT AND HISTORY OF THE PLAY

Though *Macbeth* was composed in 1605 or 1606 and apparently had its first stage production in 1606, it did not appear in print until the First Folio version in 1623. The Folio text is therefore the only authority. The duplication of a few stage directions and indications of cutting here and there suggest that the printers used a prompt copy for their text. *Macbeth* as we have it is one of Shakespeare's shortest plays and the surviving version obviously underwent drastic cutting in some of the scenes. The text printed in the Folio also shows evidence of editorial tampering and interpolation. Two songs, in Act III, Sc.v, and Act IV, Sc.i, were added from Thomas Middleton's *The Witch,* which was performed at the Blackfriars at some time before 1623. The inclusion of Middleton's songs in *Macbeth* has led some scholars to think that the play contains other interpolations by Middleton or some other hand. The scenes generally accepted as interpolations are those in which Hecate appears (III. v. and IV. i.).

Scholars have conjectured that *Macbeth* was written for the Globe and that the brevity of the surviving version is evidence of the cutting required for a later performance at Court before the King Certainly Shakespeare intended to flatter King James I by his characterization of his ancestor, Banquo. and by the dumb show of the Eight Kings with still other Stuarts to follow until Macbeth exclaims, "will the line stretch out to the crack of doom?" Since by his authorship of *Demonology* (1597) King James had shown that he was an authority on witches, scholars have seen in Shakespeare's witch scenes a subtle bit of flattery of the King There are other allusions that seem to refer to King James. That the play was presented before the King as one of the Court entertainments frequently required of Shakespeare's company is a reasonable surmise.

Macbeth remained in the repertory of the King's Men and apparently had frequent revivals. Other plays of the day show its influence. The astrologer Dr. Simon Forman saw a performance of *Macbeth* at the Globe on April 20, 1611, and wrote down a long description of his impressions in a manuscript that has survived in the

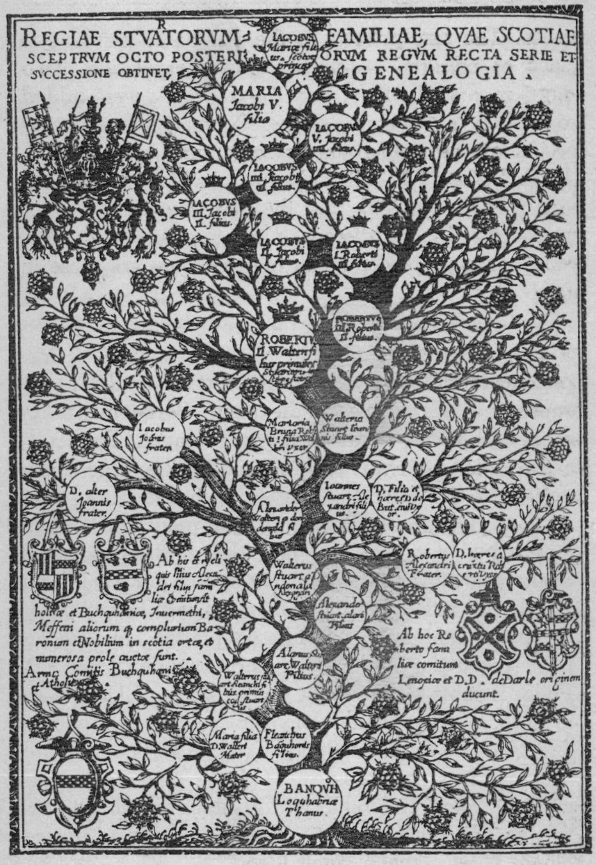

Banquo's family tree, ending in James I.

From John Leslie, *De origine, moribus, et rebus gestis Scotorum* (1578).

Bodleian Library. When the theatres were reopened after Charles II's return in 1660, *Macbeth* was one of the plays that entertained Restoration audiences, but William Davenant's adaptation of the play into a sort of opera with music, dancing, and witches flying across the stage was the version that held the stage for many years. On April 19, 1667, Samuel Pepys noted in his Diary his enjoyment of a performance of *Macbeth* "which, though I have seen it often, yet is one of the best plays for the stage, for variety of dancing and music, that ever I saw." In the late seventeenth century, Thomas Betterton found in Macbeth one of his most popular roles. His wife, who played Lady Macbeth, was succeeded in the role by Elizabeth Barry, one of the reigning favorites of the Restoration stage.

Davenant's operatic text remained the favorite version until near the middle of the eighteenth century, when, in 1744, David Garrick revised the play and restored most of Shakespeare's scenes, though he "improved" Shakespeare by writing a dying speech for Macbeth in which the villain-hero breathes his last bewailing his imminent damnation. He himself played Macbeth and later staged the play in Highland costume. When John Philip Kemble took over the management of Drury Lane in 1788, he went back to Davenant's version for operatic effects in his own production of *Macbeth.* His sister, Mrs. Siddons, made Lady Macbeth one of her most effective roles. Her rendition of the sleepwalking scene was so effective that one spectator declared, "I smelt blood! I swear that I smelt blood."

Throughout the nineteenth century, *Macbeth* was a favorite on both sides of the Atlantic. Most of the famous actors and actresses at some point played Macbeth and Lady Macbeth. Producers liked to tinker with the play for stage effects, particularly in the witch scenes. During the last half-century the popularity of *Macbeth* has remained undiminished, but modern taste is more austere and producers nowadays stick closer to Shakespeare's text. For many years *Macbeth* was one of the plays prescribed for high-school study and it has been perhaps the most widely read of Shakespeare's tragedies.

THE AUTHOR

As early as 1598 Shakespeare was so well known as a literary and dramatic craftsman that Francis Meres, in his *Palladis Tamia: Wits Treasury,* referred in flattering terms to him as "mellifluous and honey-tongued Shakespeare," famous for his *Venus and Adonis,* his *Lucrece,* and "his sugared sonnets," which were circulating "among his private friends." Meres observes further that "as Plautus and Seneca are accounted the best for comedy and tragedy among the Latins, so Shakespeare among the English is the most excellent in both kinds for the stage," and he mentions a dozen plays that had made a name for Shakespeare He concludes with the remark "that the Muses would speak with Shakespeare's fine filed phrase if they would speak English."

To those acquainted with the history of the Elizabethan and Jacobean periods, it is incredible that anyone should be so naïve or ignorant as to doubt the reality of Shakespeare as the author of the plays that bear his name. Yet so much nonsense has been written about other "candidates" for the plays that it is well to remind readers that no credible evidence that would stand up in a court of law has ever been adduced to prove either that Shakespeare did not write his plays or that anyone else wrote them. All the theories offered for the authorship of Francis Bacon, the Earl of Derby, the Earl of Oxford, the Earl of Hertford, Christopher Marlowe, and a score of other candidates are mere conjectures spun from the active imaginations of persons who confuse hypothesis and conjecture with evidence.

As Meres' statement of 1598 indicates, Shakespeare was already a popular playwright whose name carried weight at the box office. The obvious reputation of Shakespeare as early as 1598 makes the effort to prove him a myth one of the most absurd in the history of human perversity.

The anti-Shakespeareans talk darkly about a plot of vested interests to maintain the authorship of Shakespeare. Nobody has any vested interest in Shakespeare, but every scholar is interested in the truth and in the quality of evidence advanced by special pleaders who set forth hypotheses in place of facts.

The anti-Shakespeareans base their arguments upon a few simple premises, all of them false. These false premises are that Shakespeare was an unlettered yokel without any schooling, that nothing is known about Shakespeare, and that only a noble lord or the equivalent in background could have written the plays. The facts are that more is known about Shakespeare than about most dramatists of his day, that he had a very good education, acquired in the Stratford Grammar School, that the plays show no evidence of profound book learning, and that the knowledge of kings and courts evident in the plays is no greater than any intelligent young man could have picked up at second hand.

Most anti-Shakespeareans are naïve and betray an obvious snobbery. The author of their favorite plays, they imply, must have had a college diploma framed and hung on his study wall like the one in their dentist's office, and obviously so great a writer must have had a title or some equally significant evidence of exalted social background. They forget that genius has a way of cropping up in unexpected places and that none of the great creative writers of the world got his inspiration in a college or university course.

William Shakespeare was the son of John Shakespeare of Stratford-upon-Avon, a substantial citizen of that small but busy market town in the center of the rich agricultural county of Warwick. John Shakespeare kept a shop, what we would call a general store; he dealt in wool and other produce and gradually acquired property. As a youth, John Shakespeare had learned the trade of glover and leather worker. There is no contemporary evidence that the elder Shakespeare was a butcher, though the anti-Shakespeareans like to talk about the ignorant "butcher's boy of Stratford." Their only evidence is a statement by gossipy John Aubrey, more than a century after William Shakespeare's birth, that young William followed his father's trade, and when he killed a calf, "he would do it in a high style and make a speech." We would like to believe the story true, but Aubrey is not a very credible witness.

John Shakespeare probably continued to operate a farm at Snitterfield that his father had leased. He married Mary Arden, daughter of his father's landlord, a man of some property. The third of their eight children was William, baptized on April 26, 1564, and probably born three days before. At least, it is conventional to celebrate April 23 as his birthday.

The Stratford records give considerable information about John Shakespeare. We know that he held several municipal offices including those of alderman and mayor. In 1580 he was in some sort of legal difficulty and was fined for neglecting a summons of the Court of Queen's Bench requiring him to appear at Westminster and be bound over to keep the peace.

As a citizen and alderman of Stratford, John Shakespeare was entitled to send his son to the grammar school free. Though the records are lost, there can be no reason to doubt that this is where young William received his education. As any student of the period knows, the grammar schools provided the basic education in Latin learning and literature. The Elizabethan grammar school is not to be confused with modern grammar schools. Many cultivated men of the day received all their formal education in the grammar schools. At the universities in this period a student would have received little training that would have inspired him to be a creative writer. At Stratford young Shakespeare would have acquired a familiarity with Latin and some little knowledge of Greek. He would have read Latin authors and become acquainted with the plays of Plautus and Terence. Undoubtedly, in this period of his life he received that stimulation to read and explore for himself the world of ancient and modern history which he later utilized in his plays. The youngster who does not acquire this type of intellectual curiosity *before* college days rarely develops as a result of a college course the kind of mind Shakespeare demonstrated. His learning in books was anything but profound, but he clearly had the probing curiosity that sent him in search of information, and he had a keenness in the observation of nature and of humankind that finds reflection in his poetry.

There is little documentation for Shakespeare's boyhood. There is little reason why there should be. Nobody knew that he was going to be a dramatist about whom any scrap of information would be prized in the centuries to come. He was merely an active and vigorous youth of Stratford, perhaps assisting his father in his business, and no Boswell bothered to write down facts about him. The most important record that we have is a marriage license issued by the Bishop of Worcester on November 28, 1582, to permit William Shakespeare to marry Anne Hathaway, seven or eight years his senior; furthermore, the Bishop permitted the marriage after reading the banns only once instead of three times, evidence of the desire for haste. The need was explained on May 26, 1583, when the christening of Susanna, daughter of William and Anne Shakespeare, was recorded at Stratford. Two years later, on February 2, 1585, the records show the birth of twins to the Shakespeares, a boy and a girl who were christened Hamnet and Judith.

What William Shakespeare was doing in Stratford during the early years of his married life, or when he went to London, we do not know. It has been conjectured that he tried his hand at schoolteaching, but that is a mere guess. There is a legend that he left Stratford to escape a charge of poaching in the park of Sir Thomas Lucy of Charlecote, but there is no proof of this. There is also a legend that when first he came to London, he earned his living by holding horses outside a playhouse and presently was given employment inside, but there is nothing better than eighteenth-century hearsay for this. How Shakespeare broke into the London theatres as a dramatist and actor we do not know. But lack of information is not surprising, for Elizabethans did not write their autobiographies, and we know even less about the lives of many writers and some men of affairs than we know about Shakespeare. By 1592 he was so well established and popular that he incurred the envy of the dramatist and pamphleteer Robert Greene, who referred to him as an "upstart crow . . . in his own conceit the only Shake-scene in a country." From this time onward, contemporary allusions and references in legal documents enable the scholar to chart Shakespeare's career with greater accuracy than is possible with most other Elizabethan dramatists.

By 1594 Shakespeare was a member of the company of actors known as the Lord Chamberlain's Men. After the accession of James I, in 1603, the company would have the sovereign for their patron and would be known as the King's Men. During the period of its greatest prosperity, this company would have as its principal theatres the Globe and the Blackfriars. Shakespeare was both an actor and a shareholder in the company. Tradition has assigned him such acting roles as Adam in *As You Like It* and the Ghost in *Hamlet*, a modest place on the stage that suggests that he may have had other duties in the management of the company. Such conclusions, however, are based on surmise.

What we do know is that his plays were popular and that he was highly successful in his vocation. His first play may have been *The Comedy of Errors*, acted perhaps in 1591. Certainly this was one of his earliest plays.

The three parts of *Henry VI* were acted sometime between 1590 and 1592. Critics are not in agreement about precisely how much Shakespeare wrote of these three plays. *Richard III* probably dates from 1593. With this play Shakespeare captured the imagination of Elizabethan audiences, then enormously interested in historical plays. With *Richard III* Shakespeare also gave an interpretation pleasing to the Tudors of the rise to power of the grandfather of Queen Elizabeth. From this time onward, Shakespeare's plays followed on the stage in rapid succession: *Titus Andronicus, The Taming of the Shrew, The Two Gentlemen of Verona, Love's Labour's Lost, Romeo and Juliet, Richard II, A Midsummer Night's Dream, King John, The Merchant of Venice, Henry IV,* Pts. I and II, *Much Ado About Nothing, Henry V, Julius Cæsar, As You Like It, Twelfth Night, Hamlet, The Merry Wives of Windsor, All's Well That Ends Well, Measure for Measure, Othello, King Lear,* and nine others that followed before Shakespeare retired completely, about 1613.

In the course of his career in London, he made enough money to enable him to retire to Stratford with a competence. His purchase on May 4, 1597, of New Place, then the second-largest dwelling in Stratford, a "pretty house of brick and timber," with a handsome garden, indicates his increasing prosperity. There his wife and children lived while he busied himself in the London theatres. The summer before he acquired New Place, his life was darkened by the death of his only son, Hamnet, a child of eleven. In May, 1602, Shakespeare purchased one hundred and seven acres of fertile farmland near Stratford and a few months later bought a cottage and garden across the alley from New Place.

About 1611, he seems to have returned permanently to Stratford, for the next year a legal document refers to him as "William Shakespeare of Stratford-upon-Avon . . . gentleman." To achieve the desired appellation of gentleman, William Shakespeare had seen to it that the College of Heralds in 1596 granted his father a coat of arms. In one step he thus became a second-generation gentleman.

Shakespeare's daughter Susanna made a good match in 1607 with Dr. John Hall, a prominent and prosperous Stratford physician. His second daughter, Judith, did not marry until she was thirty-two years old, and then, under somewhat scandalous circumstances, she married Thomas Quiney, a Stratford vintner. On March 25, 1616, Shakespeare made his will, bequeathing his landed property to Susanna, £300 to Judith, certain sums to other relatives, and his second-best bed to his wife, Anne. Much has been made of the second-best bed, but the legacy probably indicates only that Anne liked that particular bed. Shakespeare, following the practice of the time, may have already arranged with Susanna for his wife's care. Finally, on April 23, 1616, the anniversary of his birth, William Shakespeare died, and he was buried on April 25 within the chancel of Trinity Church, as befitted an honored citizen. On August 6, 1623, a few months before the publication of the collected edition of Shakespeare's plays, Anne Shakespeare joined her husband in death.

THE PUBLICATION OF HIS PLAYS

During his lifetime Shakespeare made no effort to publish any of his plays, though eighteen appeared in print in single-play editions known as quartos. Some of these are corrupt versions known as "bad quartos." No quarto, so far as is known, had the author's approval. Plays were not considered "literature" any more than most radio and television scripts today are considered literature. Dramatists sold their plays outright to the theatrical companies and it was usually considered in the company's interest to keep plays from getting into print. To achieve a reputation as a man of letters, Shakespeare wrote his *Sonnets* and his narrative poems, *Venus and Adonis* and *The Rape of Lucrece*, but he probably never dreamed that his plays would establish his reputation as a literary genius. Only Ben Jonson, a man known for his colossal conceit, had the crust to call his plays *Works*, as he did when he published an edition in 1616. But men laughed at Ben Jonson.

After Shakespeare's death, two of his old colleagues in the King's Men, John Heminges and Henry Condell, decided that it would be a good thing to print, in more accurate versions than were then available, the plays already published and eighteen additional plays not previously published in quarto. In 1623 appeared *Mr. William Shakespeares Comedies, Histories, & Tragedies. Published according to the True Originall Copies. London. Printed by Isaac Iaggard and Ed. Blount.* This was the famous First Folio, a work that had the authority of Shakespeare's associates. The only play commonly attributed to Shakespeare that was omitted in the First Folio was *Pericles*. In their preface, "To the great Variety of Readers," Heminges and Condell state that whereas "you were abused with diverse stolen and surreptitious copies, maimed and deformed by the frauds and stealths of injurious impostors that exposed them, even those are now offered to your view cured and perfect of their limbs; and all the rest, absolute in their numbers, as he conceived them." What they used for printer's copy is one of the vexed problems of scholarship, and skilled bibliographers have devoted years of study to the question of the relation of the "copy" for the First Folio to Shakespeare's manuscripts. In some cases it is clear that the editors corrected printed quarto versions of the plays, probably by comparison with playhouse scripts. Whether these scripts were in Shakespeare's autograph is anybody's guess. No manuscript of any play in Shakespeare's handwriting has survived. Indeed, very few play manuscripts from this period by any author are extant. The Tudor and Stuart periods had not yet learned to prize autographs and authors' original manuscripts.

Since the First Folio contains eighteen plays not previously printed, it is the only source for these. For the other eighteen, which had appeared in quarto versions, the First Folio also has the authority of an edition prepared and overseen by Shakespeare's colleagues and professional associates. But since editorial standards in 1623 were far from strict, and Heminges and Condell were actors rather than editors by profession, the texts are sometimes careless. The printing and proofreading of the First Folio also left much to be desired, and some garbled passages have to be corrected and emended. The "good quarto" texts have to be taken into account in preparing a modern edition.

Because of the great popularity of Shakespeare through the centuries, the First Folio has become a prized book, but it is not a very rare one, for it is estimated that 238 copies are extant. The Folger Shakespeare Library in Washington, D.C., has seventy-nine copies of the First Folio, collected by the founder, Henry Clay Folger, who believed that a collection of as many texts as possible would reveal significant facts about the text of Shakespeare's plays. Dr. Charlton Hinman, using an ingenious machine of his own invention for mechanical collating, has made many discoveries that throw light on Shakespeare's text and on printing practices of the day.

The probability is that the First Folio of 1623 had an edition of between 1,000 and 1,250 copies. It is believed that it sold for £ 1, which made it an expensive book, for £ 1 in 1623 was equivalent to something between $40 and $50 in modern purchasing power.

During the seventeenth century, Shakespeare was sufficiently popular to warrant three later editions in folio size, the Second Folio of 1632, the Third Folio of 1663-1664, and the Fourth Folio of 1685. The Third Folio added six other plays ascribed to Shakespeare, but these are apocryphal.

THE SHAKESPEAREAN THEATRE

The theatres in which Shakespeare's plays were performed were vastly different from those we know today. The stage was a platform that jutted out into the area now occupied by the first rows of seats on the main floor, what is called the "orchestra" in America and the "pit" in England. This platform had no curtain to come down at the ends of acts and scenes. And although simple stage properties were available, the Elizabethan theatre lacked both the machinery and the elaborate movable scenery of the modern theatre. In the rear of the platform stage was a curtained area that could be used as an inner room, a tomb, or any such scene that might be required. A balcony above this inner room, and perhaps balconies on the sides of the stage, could represent the upper deck of a ship, the entry to Juliet's room, or a prison window. A trap door in the stage provided an entrance for ghosts and devils from the nether regions, and a similar trap in the canopied structure over the stage, known as the "heavens," made it possible to let down angels on a rope. These primitive stage arrangements help to account for many elements in Elizabethan plays. For example, since there was no curtain, the dramatist frequently felt the necessity of writing into his play action to clear the stage at the ends of acts and scenes. The funeral march at the end of *Hamlet* is not there merely for atmosphere; Shakespeare had to get the corpses off the stage. The lack of scenery also freed the dramatist from undue concern about the exact location of his sets, and the physical relation of his various settings to each other did not have to be worked out with the same precision as in the modern theatre.

Before London had buildings designed exclusively for theatrical entertainment, plays were given in inns and taverns. The characteristic inn of the period had an inner courtyard with rooms opening onto balconies overlooking the yard. Players could set up their temporary stages at one end of the yard and audiences could find seats on the balconies out of the weather. The poorer sort could stand or sit on the cobblestones in the yard, which was open to the sky. The first theatres followed this construction, and throughout the Elizabethan period the large public theatres had a yard in front of the stage open to the weather, with two or three tiers of covered balconies extending around the theatre. This physical structure again influenced the writing of plays. Because a dramatist wanted the actors to be heard, he frequently wrote into his play orations that could be delivered with declamatory effect. He also provided spectacle, buffoonery, and broad jests to keep the riotous groundlings in the yard entertained and quiet.

In another respect the Elizabethan theatre differed greatly from ours. It had no actresses. All women's roles were taken by boys, sometimes recruited from the boys' choirs of the London churches. Some of these youths acted their roles with great skill and the Elizabethans did not seem to be aware of any incongruity. The first actresses on the professional English stage appeared after the Restoration of Charles II, in 1660, when exiled Englishmen brought back from France practices of the French stage.

London in the Elizabethan period, as now, was the center of theatrical interest, though wandering actors from time to time traveled through the country performing in inns, halls, and the houses of the nobility. The first professional playhouse, called simply The Theatre, was erected by James Burbage, father of Shakespeare's colleague Richard Burbage, in 1576 on lands of the old Holywell Priory adjacent to Finsbury Fields, a playground and park area just north of the city walls. It had the advantage of being outside the city's jurisdiction and yet was near enough to be easily accessible. Soon after The Theatre was opened, another playhouse called The Curtain was erected in the same neighborhood. Both of these playhouses had open courtyards and were probably polygonal in shape.

About the time The Curtain opened, Richard Farrant, Master of the Children of the Chapel Royal at Windsor and of St. Paul's, conceived the idea of opening a "private" theatre in the old monastery buildings of the Blackfriars, not far from St. Paul's Cathedral in the heart of the city. This theatre was ostensibly to train the choirboys in plays for presentation at Court, but Farrant managed to present plays to paying audiences and achieved considerable success until aristocratic neighbors complained and had the theatre closed. This first Blackfriars Theatre was significant, however, because it popularized the boy actors in a professional way and it paved the way for a second theatre in the Blackfriars, which Shakespeare's company took over more than thirty years later. By the last years of the sixteenth century, London had at least six professional theatres and still others were erected during the reign of James I.

The Globe Theatre, the playhouse that most people connect with Shakespeare, was erected early in 1599 on the Bankside, the area across the Thames from the city. Its construction had a dramatic beginning, for on the night of December 28, 1598, James Burbage's sons, Cuthbert and Richard, gathered together a crew who tore down the old theatre in Holywell and carted the timbers across the river to a site that they had chosen for a new playhouse. The reason for this clandestine operation was a row with the landowner over the lease to the Holywell property. The site chosen for the Globe was another playground outside of the city's jurisdiction, a region of somewhat unsavory character. Not far away was the Bear Garden, an amphitheatre devoted to the baiting of bears and bulls. This was also the region occupied by many houses of ill fame licensed by the

Bishop of Winchester and the source of substantial revenue to him. But it was easily accessible either from London Bridge or by means of the cheap boats operated by the London watermen, and it had the great advantage of being beyond the authority of the Puritanical aldermen of London, who frowned on plays because they lured apprentices from work, filled their heads with improper ideas, and generally exerted a bad influence. The aldermen also complained that the crowds drawn together in the theatre helped to spread the plague.

The Globe was the handsomest theatre up to its time. It was a large building, apparently octagonal in shape and open like its predecessors to the sky in the center, but capable of seating a large audience in its covered balconies. To erect and operate the Globe, the Burbages organized a syndicate composed of the leading members of the dramatic company, of which Shakespeare was a member. Since it was open to the weather and depended on natural light, plays had to be given in the afternoon. This caused no hardship in the long afternoons of an English summer, but in the winter the weather was a great handicap and discouraged all except the hardiest. For that reason, in 1608 Shakespeare's company was glad to take over the lease of the second Blackfriars Theatre, a substantial, roomy hall reconstructed within the framework of the old monastery building. This theatre was protected from the weather and its stage was artificially lighted by chandeliers of candles. This became the winter playhouse for Shakespeare's company and at once proved so popular that the congestion of traffic created an embarrassing problem. Stringent regulations had to be made for the movement of coaches in the vicinity. Shakespeare's company continued to use the Globe during the summer months. In 1613 a squib fired from a cannon during a performance of *Henry VIII* fell on the thatched roof and the Globe burned to the ground. The next year it was rebuilt.

London had other famous theatres. The Rose, just west of the Globe, was built by Philip Henslowe, a semiliterate denizen of the Bankside, who became one of the most important theatrical owners and producers of the Tudor and Stuart periods. What is more important for historians, he kept a detailed account book, which provides much of our information about theatrical history in his time. Another famous theatre on the Bankside was the Swan, which a Dutch priest, Johannes de Witt, visited in 1596. The crude drawing of the stage which he made was copied by his friend Arend van Buchell; it is one of the important pieces of contemporary evidence for theatrical construction. Among the other theatres, the Fortune, north of the city, on Golding Lane, and the Red Bull, even farther away from the city, off St. John's Street, were the most popular. The Red Bull, much frequented by apprentices, favored sensational and sometimes rowdy plays.

The actors who kept all of these theatres going were organized into companies under the protection of some noble patron. Traditionally actors had enjoyed a low reputation. In some of the ordinances they were classed as vagrants; in the phraseology of the time, "rogues, vagabonds, sturdy beggars, and common players" were all listed together as undesirables. To escape penalties often meted out to these characters, organized groups of actors managed to gain the protection of various personages of high degree. In the later years of Eliza-

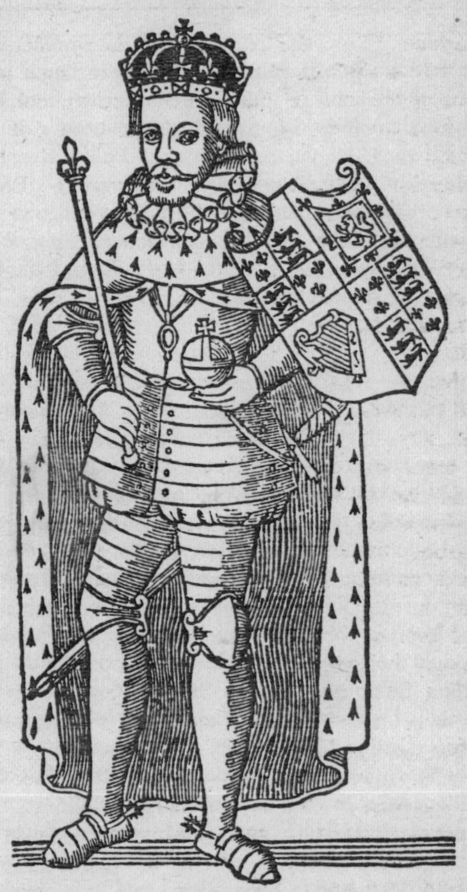

King James I.

beth's reign, a group flourished under the name of the Queen's Men; another group had the protection of the Lord Admiral and were known as the Lord Admiral's Men. Edward Alleyn, son-in-law of Philip Henslowe, was the leading spirit in the Lord Admiral's Men. Besides the adult companies, troupes of boy actors from time to time also enjoyed considerable popularity. Among these were the Children of Paul's and the Children of the Chapel Royal.

The company with which Shakespeare had a long association had for its first patron Henry Carey, Lord Hunsdon, the Lord Chamberlain, and hence they were known as the Lord Chamberlain's Men. After the accession of James I, they became the King's Men. This company was the great rival of the Lord Admiral's Men, managed by Henslowe and Alleyn.

All was not easy for the players in Shakespeare's time, for the aldermen of London were always eager for an excuse to close up the Blackfriars and any other theatres in their jurisdiction. The theatres outside the jurisdiction of London were not immune from interference, for they might be shut up by order of the Privy Council for meddling in politics or for various other offenses, or they might be closed in time of plague lest they spread infection. During plague times, the actors usually went on tour and played the provinces wherever they could find an audience. Particularly frightening were the plagues of 1592-1594 and 1613 when the theatres closed and the players, like many other Londoners, had to take to the country.

Though players had a low social status, they enjoyed great popularity, and one of the favorite forms of entertainment at Court was the performance of plays. To be commanded to perform at Court conferred great prestige upon a company of players, and printers frequently noted that fact when they published plays. Several of Shakespeare's plays were performed before the sovereign, and Shakespeare himself undoubtedly acted in some of these plays.

References for Further Reading

Many readers will want suggestions for further reading about Shakespeare and his times. The literature in this field is enormous but a few references will serve as guides to further study. A simple and useful little book is Gerald Sanders, *A Shakespeare Primer* (New York, 1950). *A Companion to Shakespeare Studies,* edited by Harley Granville-Barker and G. B. Harrison (Cambridge, Eng., 1934) is a valuable guide. More detailed but still not so voluminous as to be confusing is Hazelton Spencer, *The Art and Life of William Shakespeare* (New York, 1940) which, like Sanders' handbook, contains a brief annotated list of useful books on various aspects of the subject. The most detailed and scholarly work providing complete factual information about Shakespeare is Sir Edmund Chambers, *William Shakespeare: A Study of Facts and Problems* (2 vols., Oxford, 1930). For detailed, factual information about the Elizabethan and seventeenth-century stages, the definitive reference works are Sir Edmund Chambers, *The Elizabethan Stage* (4 vols., Oxford, 1923) and Gerald E. Bentley, *The Jacobean and Caroline Stage* (5 vols., Oxford, 1941–1956). Alfred Harbage, *Shakespeare's Audience* (New York, 1941) throws light on the nature and tastes of the customers for whom Elizabethan dramatists wrote.

Although specialists disagree about details of stage

construction, the reader will find essential information in John C. Adams, *The Globe Playhouse. Its Design and Equipment* (Barnes & Noble, 1961). A model of the Globe playhouse by Dr. Adams is on permanent exhibition in the Folger Shakespeare Library in Washington, D.C. An excellent description of the architecture of the Globe is Irwin Smith, *Shakespeare's Globe Playhouse: A Modern Reconstruction in Text and Scale Drawings Based upon the Reconstruction of the Globe by John Cranford Adams* (New York, 1956). Another recent study of the physical characteristics of the Globe is C. Walter Hodges, *The Globe Restored* (London, 1953). An easily read history of the early theatres is J. Q. Adams, *Shakespearean Playhouses: A History of English Theatres from the Beginnings to the Restoration* (Boston, 1917).

The following titles on theatrical history will provide information about Shakespeare's plays in later periods: Alfred Harbage, *Theatre for Shakespeare* (Toronto, 1955); Esther Cloudman Dunn, *Shakespeare in America* (New York, 1939); George C. D. Odell, *Shakespeare from Betterton to Irving* (2 vols., London, 1931); Arthur Colby Sprague, *Shakespeare and the Actors: The Stage Business in His Plays (1660–1905)* (Cambridge, Mass., 1944) and *Shakespearian Players and Performances* (Cambridge, Mass., 1953); Leslie Hotson, *The Commonwealth and Restoration Stage* (Cambridge, Mass., 1928); Alwin Thaler, *Shakspere to Sheridan: A Book About the Theatre of Yesterday and To-day* (Cambridge, Mass., 1922); Ernest Bradlee Watson, *Sheridan to Robertson: A Study of the 19th-Century London Stage* (Cambridge, Mass., 1926). Enid Welsford, *The Court Masque* (Cambridge, Mass., 1927) is an excellent study of the characteristics of this form of entertainment.

Harley Granville-Barker, *Prefaces to Shakespeare* (5 vols., London, 1927–1948) provides stimulating critical discussion of the plays. An older classic of criticism is Andrew C. Bradley, *Shakespearean Tragedy: Lectures on Hamlet, Othello, King Lear, Macbeth* (London, 1904), which is now available in an inexpensive reprint (New York, 1955).

The question of the authenticity of Shakespeare's plays arouses perennial attention. A book that demolishes the notion of hidden cryptograms in the plays is William F. Friedman and Elizebeth S. Friedman, *The Shakespearean Ciphers Examined* (New York, 1957). Other useful works are: R. C. Churchill, *Shakespeare and His Betters* (Bloomington, Ind., 1959) and Frank W. Wadsworth, *The Poacher from Stratford: A Partial Account of the Controversy over the Authorship of Shakespeare's Plays* (Berkeley, Calif., 1958), Louis B. Wright, "The Anti-Shakespeare Industry and the Growth of Cults," *The Virginia Quarterly Review*, XXXV (1959), 289-303. A recent treatment of this theme is *The Authorship of Shakespeare*, by James G. McManaway, in the Folger Library series of "Booklets on Tudor and Stuart Civilization" (Washington, 1962).

Much background information about Scottish history and Shakespeare's flattery of King James in *Macbeth* is to be found in Henry N. Paul, *The Royal Play of Macbeth* (New York, 1950). One of the best and most sensible of the recent discussions of *Macbeth* is to be found in Kenneth Muir's introduction to the new Arden edition, published by Harvard in 1953. Miss Lily Bess Campbell gives a provocative analysis of *Macbeth* and the influence of fear upon him in *Shakespeare's Tragic Heroes* (New York, 1930).

A brief, clear, and accurate account of Tudor history is S. T. Bindoff, *The Tudors,* in the Penguin series. A readable general history is G. M. Trevelyan, *The History of England* first published in 1926 and available in many editions. G. M. Trevelyan, *English Social History,* first published in 1942 and also available in many editions, provides fascinating information about England in all periods. Sir John Neale, *Queen Elizabeth* (London, 1934) is the best study of the great Queen. Various aspects of life in the Elizabethan period are treated in Louis B. Wright, *Middle Class Culture in Elizabethan England* (Chapel Hill, N.C., 1935; reprinted by Cornell University Press, 1958). *Shakespeare's England: An Account of the Life and Manners of His Age* edited by Sidney Lee and C. T. Onions (2 vols., Oxford, 1916), provides a large amount of information on many aspects of life in the Elizabethan period. Additional information will be found in Muriel St. C. Byrne, *Elizabethan Life in Town and Country* (Barnes & Noble, 1961).

The Folger Shakespeare Library is currently publishing a series of illustrated pamphlets on various aspects of English life in the sixteenth and seventeenth century. Among the titles in print are *Shakespeare's Theatre and the Dramatic Tradition,* by Louis B. Wright, and *The Life of William Shakespeare* by Giles E. Dawson.

[*Dramatis Personae.*

Duncan, King of Scotland.

Malcolm, *Donalbain*, his sons.

Macbeth, *Banquo*, Generals of the Scottish Army.

Macduff, *Lennox*, *Ross*, *Menteith*, *Angus*, *Caithness*, Noblemen of Scotland.

Fleance, son to *Banquo*.

Siward, Earl of Northumberland, General of the English forces.

Young Siward, his son.

Seyton, an Officer attending on *Macbeth*.

Boy, son to *Macduff*.

A Captain.

An English Doctor.

A Scottish Doctor.

A Porter.

An Old Man.

Lady Macbeth.
Lady Macduff.
A Gentlewoman, attending on *Lady Macbeth.*

Hecate.
Three Witches.
The Ghost of *Banquo.*
Apparitions.

Lords, Gentlemen, Officers, Soldiers, Murderers, Messengers, Attendants.

SCENE: *Scotland and England.*]

THE TRAGEDY OF

MACBETH

ACT I

I. i. The three witches set the tone of the play as they wait for Macbeth.

9. **Graymalkin:** a common name for a domestic cat, here apparently the First Witch's familiar; that is, a demon serving her in the form of a cat.

10. **Paddock:** a toad, the familiar of the Second Witch.

I. ii. Duncan, King of Scotland, receives a report of a victory over a Norwegian invader of his kingdom and a local rebellion. To his kinsman Macbeth goes the principal credit for the victory of his forces. Duncan orders the execution of the Thane of Cawdor for disloyalty, and invests Macbeth with his title.

Stage Dir. **Alarum:** a trumpet call to arms.

Kerns and gallowglasses.

From an 1883 reprint of John Derricke, *The Image of Ireland* (1581).

ACT I

Scene I. [Scotland. An open place.]

Thunder and lightning. Enter three *Witches.*

1. Witch. When shall we three meet again
In thunder, lightning, or in rain?
2. Witch. When the hurlyburly's done,
When the battle's lost and won.
3. Witch. That will be ere the set of sun.
1. Witch. Where the place?
2. Witch. Upon the heath.
3. Witch. There to meet with Macbeth.
1. Witch. I come, Graymalkin!
2. Witch. Paddock calls.
3. Witch. Anon!
All. Fair is foul, and foul is fair.
Hover through the fog and filthy air.

Exeunt.

Scene II. [A camp near Forres.]

Alarum within. Enter *King* [*Duncan*], *Malcolm, Donalbain, Lennox,* with *Attendants,* meeting a bleeding *Captain.*

King. What bloody man is that? He can report,

4. **sergeant:** an officer attendant upon a knight in the field.

11. **choke their art:** prevent each other from exercising their skill.

12. **to that:** i.e., to that end (of becoming a rebel).

15. **kerns:** light-armed, undisciplined foot soldiers, usually designating Irish soldiers, but sometimes applied to Scottish Highlanders; **gallowglasses:** soldiers more heavily armed and better trained than **kerns.**

16. **damned:** accursed, because treasonous.

17. **whore:** the fickleness of the goddess Fortune was a proverbial idea which earned her the name of **whore** more than once in Elizabethan writings; **all's too weak:** all Macdonwald and his forces can do, with Fortune favoring their cause, is not enough.

21. **valor's minion:** the darling or favorite of valor personified.

24. **unseamed him from the nave to the chops:** laid him open from navel to jaws.

27. **whence the sun 'gins his reflection:** i.e., the east.

28. **thunders break:** the First Folio has no verb in the sentence. Alexander Pope suggested "break," adapting the Second Folio's "breaking."

As seemeth by his plight, of the revolt
The newest state.
Mal. This is the sergeant
Who like a good and hardy soldier fought
'Gainst my captivity. Hail, brave friend!
Say to the King the knowledge of the broil
As thou didst leave it.
Capt. Doubtful it stood,
As two spent swimmers that do cling together
And choke their art. The merciless Macdonwald
(Worthy to be a rebel, for to that
The multiplying villainies of nature
Do swarm upon him) from the Western Isles
Of kerns and gallowglasses is supplied;
And Fortune, on his damned quarrel smiling,
Showed like a rebel's whore. But all's too weak;
For brave Macbeth (well he deserves that name),
Disdaining Fortune, with his brandished steel,
Which smoked with bloody execution
(Like valor's minion), carved out his passage
Till he faced the slave;
Which ne'er shook hands nor bade farewell to him
Till he unseamed him from the nave to the chops
And fixed his head upon our battlements.
King. O valiant cousin! worthy gentleman!
Capt. As whence the sun 'gins his reflection
Shipwracking storms and direful thunders break,
So from that spring whence comfort seemed to come
Discomfort swells. Mark, King of Scotland, mark.
No sooner justice had, with valor armed,
Compelled these skipping kerns to trust their heels

33. **the Norweyan lord:** the King of Norway; **surveying vantage:** seeing a favorable opportunity.

40. **sooth:** truth.

41. **overcharged with double cracks:** overloaded with two balls at once.

44. **memorize another Golgotha:** make the place as memorable for slaughter as the Biblical Golgotha where Christ was crucified.

50. **Thane:** chief of a clan, ranking with the son of an earl.

57. **flout:** defy.

58. **fan our people cold:** chill our men with fear; **Norway himself:** the King of Norway.

Mars (Bellona's bridegroom).
From R. Whitcombe, *Janua divorum* (1678).

But the Norweyan lord, surveying vantage,
With furbished arms and new supplies of men,
Began a fresh assault.
King. Dismayed not this
Our captains, Macbeth and Banquo?
Capt. Yes,
As sparrows eagles, or the hare the lion.
If I say sooth I must report they were
As cannons overcharged with double cracks, so they
Doubly redoubled strokes upon the foe.
Except they meant to bathe in reeking wounds,
Or memorize another Golgotha,
I cannot tell–
But I am faint; my gashes cry for help.
King. So well thy words become thee as thy wounds;
They smack of honor both. Go get him surgeons.
[*Exit Captain, attended.*]

Enter *Ross* and *Angus.*

Who comes here?
Mal. The worthy Thane of Ross.
Len. What a haste looks through his eyes! So should he look
That seems to speak things strange.
Ross. God save the King!
King. Whence cam'st thou, worthy thane?
Ross. From Fife, great King,
Where the Norweyan banners flout the sky
And fan our people cold. Norway himself,
With terrible numbers,

61. **a dismal conflict:** a battle that appeared to be unlucky for the Scots.

62. **Bellona's bridegroom:** the spouse of the Roman goddess of war, sometimes identified as Mars himself. Macbeth is meant; **proof:** strong armor, proof against penetration.

63. **Confronted him with self-comparisons:** defied him and matched his prowess.

65. **lavish:** undisciplined.

69. **composition:** a treaty.

71. **Saint Colme's Inch:** now known as Inchcolm in the Firth of Forth, the island of Saint Columba, an Irish monk who founded many monasteries in Scotland and the Hebrides.

74. **Our bosom interest:** my dearest concerns; **present:** immediate.

I. iii. Macbeth and Banquo encounter the three witches, who hail Macbeth as Thane of Glamis (his present title), Thane of Cawdor, and "King hereafter." They add the prophecy that Banquo will beget kings; then they vanish. While Macbeth and Banquo are wondering at their words, they are joined by Ross and Angus who bring the King's thanks for their successful defense of his kingdom and inform Macbeth of his new title of Thane of Cawdor. This partial confirmation of the witches' words moves Macbeth deeply and it is clear that ambition is tempting him to seek the greater honor also promised him.

Assisted by that most disloyal traitor
The Thane of Cawdor, began a dismal conflict,
Till that Bellona's bridegroom, lapped in proof,
Confronted him with self-comparisons,
Point against point, rebellious arm 'gainst arm,
Curbing his lavish spirit; and to conclude,
The victory fell on us.
King. Great happiness!
Ross. That now
Sweno, the Norways' king, craves composition;
Nor would we deign him burial of his men
Till he disbursed, at Saint Colme's Inch,
Ten thousand dollars to our general use.
King. No more that Thane of Cawdor shall deceive
Our bosom interest. Go pronounce his present death
And with his former title greet Macbeth.
Ross. I'll see it done.
Dun. What he hath lost noble Macbeth hath won.
Exeunt.

Scene III. [A heath near Forres.]

Thunder. Enter the three *Witches.*

1. *Witch.* Where hast thou been, sister?
2. *Witch.* Killing swine.
3. *Witch.* Sister, where thou?
1. *Witch.* A sailor's wife had chestnuts in her lap
And mounched and mounched and mounched. "Give me," quoth I.

7. **Aroint thee:** be off with you; **rump-fed:** fat-rumped; **ronyon:** good-for-nothing.

8. **Her husband's to Aleppo gone, master o' the "Tiger": Aleppo** in Syria was famous in Shakespeare's age as a trading center for the Levant Company. The name "Tiger" was used for several merchant ships.

10. **like a rat without a tail:** in the form of a tailless rat.

18. **shipman's card:** navigator's compass or chart; **card** was used for both the compass card on which the points were marked and the geographical chart used in navigation.

21. **penthouse lid:** eyelid.

22. **forbid:** accursed.

24. **peak:** synonymous with **dwindle** and **pine.**

33. **The Weird Sisters:** the Folio has "weyward" here and at I. v. 7 and II. i. 25, elsewhere "weyard." Lewis Theobald suggested **weird,** from the Old English *wyrd,* a form of the verb "to become." Applied to the three witches, it associates them with the classical Fates and the Norns of Norse mythology. Holinshed says that "the common opinion" after Macbeth's career was known was that they were "the weird sisters, that is . . . the goddesses of destiny." It is likely, however, that Shakespeare conceived them in contemporary terms and intended them to be no more than typical witches posing as Fates in order to entrap Macbeth.

34. **Posters:** speedy travelers.

"Aroint thee, witch!" the rump-fed ronyon cries.
Her husband's to Aleppo gone, master o' the "Tiger";
But in a sieve I'll thither sail
And, like a rat without a tail,
I'll do, I'll do, and I'll do.
2. Witch I'll give thee a wind.
1. Witch. Th' art kind.
3. Witch. And I another.
1. Witch. I myself have all the other,
And the very ports they blow,
All the quarters that they know
I' the shipman's card.
I'll drain him dry as hay.
Sleep shall neither night nor day
Hang upon his penthouse lid.
He shall live a man forbid.
Weary sev'nights, nine times nine,
Shall he dwindle, peak, and pine.
Though his bark cannot be lost,
Yet it shall be tempest-tost.
Look what I have.
2. Witch. Show me! show me!
1. Witch. Here I have a pilot's thumb,
Wracked as homeward he did come.
Drum within.
3. Witch. A drum, a drum!
Macbeth doth come.
All. The Weird Sisters, hand in hand,
Posters of the sea and land,
Thus do go about, about,
Thrice to thine, and thrice to mine,

45. **choppy:** chapped.

46. **You should be:** you must be (considering the rest of your features).

58. **fantastical:** figments of fancy, illusions.

60. **present:** immediate; see I. ii. 74; **grace:** honor.

A vessel "tempest-tost."

From Holinshed, *The Historie of Scotland* . . . (1577).

And thrice again, to make up nine.
Peace! The charm's wound up.

Enter *Macbeth* and *Banquo*.

Macb. So foul and fair a day I have not seen.
Ban. How far is't called to Forres? What are these,
So withered, and so wild in their attire,
That look not like the inhabitants o' the earth,
And yet are on't? Live you? or are you aught
That man may question? You seem to understand me,
By each at once her choppy finger laying
Upon her skinny lips. You should be women,
And yet your beards forbid me to interpret
That you are so.
Macb. Speak, if you can. What are you?
1. Witch. All hail, Macbeth! Hail to thee, Thane of Glamis!
2. Witch. All hail, Macbeth! Hail to thee, Thane of Cawdor!
3. Witch. All hail, Macbeth, that shalt be King hereafter!
Ban. Good sir, why do you start and seem to fear
Things that do sound so fair? I' the name of truth,
Are ye fantastical, or that indeed
Which outwardly ye show? My noble partner
You greet with present grace and great prediction
Of noble having and of royal hope,
That he seems rapt withal. To me you speak not.
If you can look into the seeds of time
And say which grain will grow and which will not,

72. **get:** beget.

76. **Sinel:** Macbeth's father.

81. **owe:** possess.

89-90. **the insane root/ That takes the reason prisoner:** a number of plants were said to cause insanity, among them hemlock and henbane.

The meeting with the three witches.

From Holinshed, *The Historie of Scotland . . .* (1577).

Speak then to me, who neither beg nor fear
Your favors nor your hate.

1. Witch. Hail!

2. Witch. Hail!

3. Witch. Hail!

1. Witch. Lesser than Macbeth, and greater.

2. Witch. Not so happy, yet much happier.

3. Witch. Thou shalt get kings, though thou be none.
So all hail, Macbeth and Banquo!

1. Witch. Banquo and Macbeth, all hail!

Macb. Stay, you imperfect speakers, tell me more!
By Sinel's death I know I am Thane of Glamis,
But how of Cawdor? The Thane of Cawdor lives,
A prosperous gentleman; and to be King
Stands not within the prospect of belief,
No more than to be Cawdor. Say from whence
You owe this strange intelligence, or why
Upon this blasted heath you stop our way
With such prophetic greeting. Speak, I charge you.

Witches vanish.

Ban. The earth hath bubbles, as the water has,
And these are of them. Whither are they vanished?

Macb. Into the air, and what seemed corporal melted
As breath into the wind. Would they had stayed!

Ban. Were such things here as we do speak about?
Or have we eaten on the insane root
That takes the reason prisoner?

Macb. Your children shall be kings.

Ban. You shall be King.

Macb. And Thane of Cawdor too. Went it not so?

Ban. To the selfsame tune and words. Who's here?

98-9. **His wonders and his praises do contend/ Which should be thine or his:** his wonder is so great as to leave him speechless so that he cannot sing your praise.

104. **post with post:** that is, messengers followed closely on each other's heels.

111. **earnest:** partial payment to seal an agreement; thus, an immediate sample of greater honor to come.

113. **addition:** title.

121. **line the rebel:** reinforce the rebellious Macdonwald.

122. **vantage:** advantage; synonymous with **help;** see I. ii. 33.

Macbeth leading Duncan's forces.

From Olaus Magnus, *Historia de gentibus septentrionalibus* (1555).

Enter *Ross* and *Angus*.

Ross. The King hath happily received, Macbeth,
The news of thy success; and when he reads
Thy personal venture in the rebels' fight,
His wonders and his praises do contend
Which should be thine or his. Silenced with that,
In viewing o'er the rest o' the selfsame day,
He finds thee in the stout Norweyan ranks,
Nothing afeard of what thyself didst make,
Strange images of death. As thick as hail
Came post with post, and every one did bear
Thy praises in his kingdom's great defense
And poured them down before him.
Ang. We are sent
To give thee from our royal master thanks;
Only to herald thee into his sight,
Not pay thee.
Ross. And for an earnest of a greater honor,
He bade me, from him, call thee Thane of Cawdor;
In which addition, hail, most worthy Thane!
For it is thine.
Ban. What, can the devil speak true?
Macb. The Thane of Cawdor lives. Why do you dress me
In borrowed robes?
Ang. Who was the Thane lives yet,
But under heavy judgment bears that life
Which he deserves to lose. Whether he was combined
With those of Norway, or did line the rebel
With hidden help and vantage, or that with both

123. **wrack:** ruin.

124. **treasons capital:** capital treasons; that is, treasons meriting the death penalty.

127. **behind:** to follow.

133. **home:** to the limit.

134. **enkindle you unto:** encourage you to hope for.

138. **betray's:** betray us.

139. **In deepest consequence:** in the particular event that means most to us.

142. **swelling:** magnificent, stately.

146. **earnest:** tangible evidence; see l. 111.

150. **seated:** fixed.

151. **Against the use of nature:** i.e., unnaturally; **Present fears:** immediate fears prompted by actual situations.

153. **yet is but fantastical:** exists so far only in the mind; see l. 58.

He labored in his country's wrack, I know not;
But treasons capital, confessed and proved,
Have overthrown him.
Macb. [*Aside*] Glamis, and Thane of Cawdor!
The greatest is behind.—[*To Ross and Angus*] Thanks for your pains.
[*Aside to Banquo*] Do you not hope your children shall be kings,
When those that gave the Thane of Cawdor to me
Promised no less to them?
Ban. [*Aside to Macbeth*] That, trusted home,
Might yet enkindle you unto the crown,
Besides the Thane of Cawdor. But 'tis strange!
And oftentimes, to win us to our harm,
The instruments of darkness tell us truths,
Win us with honest trifles, to betray's
In deepest consequence.—
Cousins, a word, I pray you.
Macb. [*Aside*] Two truths are told,
As happy prologues to the swelling act
Of the imperial theme.—I thank you, gentlemen.—
[*Aside*] This supernatural soliciting
Cannot be ill; cannot be good. If ill,
Why hath it given me earnest of success,
Commencing in a truth? I am Thane of Cawdor.
If good, why do I yield to that suggestion
Whose horrid image doth unfix my hair
And make my seated heart knock at my ribs
Against the use of nature? Present fears
Are less than horrible imaginings.
My thought, whose murder yet is but fantastical,

154. **single:** undivided, not torn by conflict.

154-56. **function/ Is smothered in surmise and nothing is/ But what is not:** the normal functioning of my mind and body is overpowered by speculation and nothing seems real but the imagined future.

161-63. **New honors come upon him,/ Like our strange garments, cleave not to their mold/ But with the aid of use:** new honors having come to him resemble human clothing, which does not seem to fit properly until it becomes habitual.

166. **stay:** wait.

167. **favor:** indulgence; that is, excuse me; **wrought:** wrought up.

169-70. **registered where every day I turn/ The leaf to read them:** that is, recorded in my mind.

172. **at more time:** when we have more time.

173. **The interim having weighed it:** having used the intervening time to consider it.

174. **free:** frank.

Shakes so my single state of man that function
Is smothered in surmise and nothing is
But what is not.

Ban. Look how our partner's rapt.

Macb. [*Aside*] If chance will have me King, why, chance may crown me,
Without my stir.

Ban. New honors come upon him,
Like our strange garments, cleave not to their mold
But with the aid of use.

Macb. [*Aside*] Come what come may,
Time and the hour runs through the roughest day.

Ban. Worthy Macbeth, we stay upon your leisure.

Macb. Give me your favor. My dull brain was wrought
With things forgotten. Kind gentlemen, your pains
Are registered where every day I turn
The leaf to read them. Let us toward the King.
[*Aside to Banquo*] Think upon what hath chanced, and, at more time,
The interim having weighed it, let us speak
Our free hearts each to other.

Ban. [*Aside to Macbeth*] Very gladly.

Macb. [*Aside to Banquo*] Till then, enough.—Come, friends.

Exeunt.

I. iv. King Duncan receives news of the Thane of Cawdor's execution, preceded by his full confession and repentance. Macbeth, Banquo, Ross and Angus enter and the King expresses his gratitude. In the next breath he names his son Malcolm as heir to the throne and indicates his intention of visiting Macbeth at Inverness. Macbeth departs to prepare his household for the visit. Already his thoughts are on murder.

2. **Those in commission:** the agents of the execution.

10. **studied:** rehearsed.

11. **owed:** owned; see I. iii. 81.

14. **To find the mind's construction in the face:** to interpret how the mind may be working by a man's appearance.

18-9. **even now/ Was heavy on me:** that is, it has just been causing me deep concern.

Scene IV. [Forres. The Palace.]

Flourish. Enter *King* [*Duncan*], *Lennox, Malcolm, Donalbain,* and *Attendants.*

King. Is execution done on Cawdor? Are not
Those in commission yet returned?
Mal. My liege,
They are not yet come back. But I have spoke
With one that saw him die; who did report
That very frankly he confessed his treasons,
Implored your Highness' pardon, and set forth
A deep repentance. Nothing in his life
Became him like the leaving it. He died
As one that had been studied in his death
To throw away the dearest thing he owed
As 'twere a careless trifle.
King. There's no art
To find the mind's construction in the face.
He was a gentleman on whom I built
An absolute trust.

Enter *Macbeth, Banquo, Ross,* and *Angus.*

O worthiest cousin,
The sin of my ingratitude even now
Was heavy on me! Thou art so far before
That swiftest wing of recompense is slow
To overtake thee. Would thou hadst less deserved,

22-3. **the proportion both of thanks and payment/ Might have been mine:** my thanks and payment might have exceeded your deserts.

40. **Wanton:** unrestrained.

43. **estate:** that is, the throne.

48. **Inverness:** Macbeth's castle.

50. **rest:** leisure.

51. **harbinger:** officer who precedes royalty and arranges proper entertainment for a visit.

The execution of the Thane of Cawdor.

From Holinshed, *The Historie of Scotland* . . . (1577).

That the proportion both of thanks and payment
Might have been mine! Only I have left to say,
More is thy due than more than all can pay.
Macb. The service and the loyalty I owe,
In doing it pays itself. Your Highness' part
Is to receive our duties; and our duties
Are to your throne and state children and servants,
Which do but what they should by doing everything
Safe toward your love and honor.
King. Welcome hither.
I have begun to plant thee and will labor
To make thee full of growing. Noble Banquo,
That hast no less deserved, nor must be known
No less to have done so, let me infold thee
And hold thee to my heart.
Ban. There if I grow,
The harvest is your own.
King. My plenteous joys,
Wanton in fullness, seek to hide themselves
In drops of sorrow. Sons, kinsmen, thanes,
And you whose places are the nearest, know
We will establish our estate upon
Our eldest, Malcolm, whom we name hereafter
The Prince of Cumberland; which honor must
Not unaccompanied invest him only,
But signs of nobleness, like stars, shall shine
On all deservers. From hence to Inverness,
And bind us further to you.
Macb. The rest is labor, which is not used for you.
I'll be myself the harbinger, and make joyful

60. **wink at:** deliberately close to avoid seeing.

62. **full so:** every bit as brave (as Banquo has just said he was).

I. v. Lady Macbeth reads a letter from her husband telling her of the meeting with the witches and the fulfillment of their first prophecy. She is determined that Macbeth shall achieve the crown, though she fears he must be urged on to take the necessary action. A messenger informs her of the King's impending visit and she invokes the powers of evil to help her stifle feminine weakness which might interfere with her resolution to see that his murder is accomplished. Macbeth enters and she greets him in exalted tones, speaking of Duncan's murder as a foregone conclusion.

---

6. **missives:** messengers.

The hearing of my wife with your approach;
So, humbly take my leave.

King. My worthy Cawdor!

Macb. [*Aside*] The Prince of Cumberland! That is a step
On which I must fall down, or else o'erleap,
For in my way it lies. Stars, hide your fires!
Let not light see my black and deep desires.
The eye wink at the hand; yet let that be,
Which the eye fears, when it is done, to see. *Exit.*

King. True, worthy Banquo: he is full so valiant,
And in his commendations I am fed;
It is a banquet to me. Let's after him,
Whose care is gone before to bid us welcome.
It is a peerless kinsman.

Flourish. Exeunt.

Scene V. [Inverness. Macbeth's Castle.]

Enter *Macbeth's Wife,* alone, with a letter.

Lady. [*Reads*] "They met me in the day of success; and I have learned by the perfect'st report they have more in them than mortal knowledge. When I burned in desire to question them further, they made themselves air, into which they vanished. Whiles I stood rapt in the wonder of it, came missives from the King, who all-hailed me Thane of Cawdor, by which title, before, these Weird Sisters saluted me, and referred me to the coming on of

19. **illness:** the wicked quality of being unscrupulous.

21. **wouldst wrongly win:** i.e., he yearns for what he can only acquire by wrongdoing.

24. **that:** i.e., Duncan's death.

25. **Hie:** hurry.

28. **golden round:** the crown of Scotland.

29. **metaphysical:** supernatural.

time with 'Hail, King that shalt be!' This have I thought good to deliver thee, my dearest partner of greatness, that thou mightst not lose the dues of rejoicing by being ignorant of what greatness is promised thee. Lay it to thy heart, and farewell."

Glamis thou art, and Cawdor, and shalt be
What thou art promised. Yet do I fear thy nature.
It is too full o' the milk of human kindness
To catch the nearest way. Thou wouldst be great;
Art not without ambition, but without
The illness should attend it. What thou wouldst highly,
That wouldst thou holily; wouldst not play false,
And yet wouldst wrongly win. Thou'ldst have, great Glamis,
That which cries "Thus thou must do," if thou have it;
And that which rather thou dost fear to do
Than wishest should be undone. Hie thee hither,
That I may pour my spirits in thine ear
And chastise with the valor of my tongue
All that impedes thee from the golden round
Which fate and metaphysical aid doth seem
To have thee crowned withal.

Enter *Messenger*.

What is your tidings?

Mess. The King comes here tonight.

Lady. Thou'rt mad to say it!
Is not thy master with him? who, were't so,
Would have informed for preparation.

37. **had the speed of him:** surpassed him in speed.

42. **The raven himself is hoarse:** the raven's voice is hoarser than usual at announcing an arrival that means death.

45. **mortal:** deadly.

49. **compunctious visitings of nature:** natural pangs of conscience.

50. **fell:** savage, deadly.

50-1. **keep peace between/ The effect and it:** that is, prevent compassionate instinct from canceling her murderous intention.

53. **sightless:** unseen, invisible.

55. **pall:** shroud: **dunnest:** darkest.

Mess. So please you, it is true. Our Thane is coming.
One of my fellows had the speed of him,
Who, almost dead for breath, had scarcely more
Than would make up his message.
Lady. Give him tending;
He brings great news.

Exit Messenger.

The raven himself is hoarse
That croaks the fatal entrance of Duncan
Under my battlements. Come, you spirits
That tend on mortal thoughts, unsex me here,
And fill me, from the crown to the toe, top-full
Of direst cruelty! Make thick my blood;
Stop up the access and passage to remorse,
That no compunctious visitings of nature
Shake my fell purpose nor keep peace between
The effect and it! Come to my woman's breasts
And take my milk for gall, you murd'ring ministers,
Wherever in your sightless substances
You wait on nature's mischief! Come, thick night,
And pall thee in the dunnest smoke of hell,
That my keen knife see not the wound it makes,
Nor heaven peep through the blanket of the dark
To cry "Hold, hold!"

Enter *Macbeth.*

Great Glamis! worthy Cawdor!
Greater than both, by the all-hail hereafter!
Thy letters have transported me beyond

62. **ignorant present: ignorant** because unaware of the future.

63. **in the instant:** at this very moment.

71-2. **To beguile the time,/ Look like the time:** to fool the multitude, behave as occasion demands.

76. **dispatch:** contrivance.

77-8. **Which shall . . . / Give solely sovereign sway and masterdom:** that is, the accomplishment of **This night's great business** will result in the acquisition of royal power for themselves.

80. **clear:** innocent.

81. **To alter favor ever is to fear:** to change countenance is to show fear.

I. vi. King Duncan and his party arrive at Macbeth's castle and are greeted by Lady Macbeth with false professions of duty and welcome.

Entrance. **Hautboys:** oboes.

This ignorant present, and I feel now
The future in the instant.
Macb. My dearest love,
Duncan comes here tonight.
Lady. And when goes hence?
Macb. Tomorrow, as he purposes.
Lady. O, never
Shall sun that morrow see!
Your face, my Thane, is as a book where men
May read strange matters. To beguile the time,
Look like the time; bear welcome in your eye,
Your hand, your tongue; look like the innocent flower,
But be the serpent under't. He that's coming
Must be provided for; and you shall put
This night's great business into my dispatch,
Which shall to all our nights and days to come
Give solely sovereign sway and masterdom.
Macb. We will speak further.
Lady. Only look up clear.
To alter favor ever is to fear.
Leave all the rest to me.

Exeunt.

Scene VI. [The same. Before Macbeth's Castle.]

Hautboys and torches. Enter *King* [*Duncan*], *Malcolm, Donalbain, Banquo, Lennox, Macduff, Ross, Angus,* and *Attendants.*

King. This castle hath a pleasant seat. The air

3. **gentle:** gentled; that is, soothed.

5. **martlet:** house martin; a bird of the swallow family; **approve:** demonstrate.

6. **loved mansionry:** favorite nesting place.

7. **jutty:** projection.

8. **coign of vantage:** suitable corner.

9. **procreant:** breeding.

13-4. **The love that follows us sometime is our trouble,/ Which still we thank as love:** though human love is sometimes troublesome, we are always grateful to have it.

15-6. **'ield us for your pains/ And thank us for your trouble: 'ield** (yield) means reward. Duncan points out that he is the one to be rewarded and thanked because the trouble he is causing his hosts is the result of the love that prompts his visit. **Us** is the royal plural.

19. **single:** weak, inadequate.

23. **rest:** remain; **hermits:** beadsmen (folk who repaid benefactors with their prayers).

25. **coursed him at the heels:** pursued him closely.

26. **purveyor:** one who makes advance arrangements for a royal party. Duncan suggests here the great favor that he wishes to show Macbeth.

27. **holp:** helped.

Nimbly and sweetly recommends itself
Unto our gentle senses.
Ban. This guest of summer,
The temple-haunting martlet, does approve
By his loved mansionry that the heaven's breath
Smells wooingly here. No jutty, frieze,
Buttress, nor coign of vantage, but this bird
Hath made his pendent bed and procreant cradle.
Where they most breed and haunt, I have observed
The air is delicate.

Enter *Lady* [*Macbeth*].

King. See, see, our honored hostess!
The love that follows us sometime is our trouble,
Which still we thank as love. Herein I teach you
How you shall bid God 'ield us for your pains
And thank us for your trouble.
Lady. All our service
In every point twice done, and then done double,
Were poor and single business to contend
Against those honors deep and broad wherewith
Your Majesty loads our house. For those of old,
And the late dignities heaped up to them,
We rest your hermits.
King. Where's the Thane of Cawdor?
We coursed him at the heels and had a purpose
To be his purveyor; but he rides well,
And his great love, sharp as his spur, hath holp him
To his home before us. Fair and noble hostess,
We are your guest tonight.

31. **compt:** trust.

33. **Still:** ever; whenever demanded; see l. 14.

37. **By your leave:** with your permission.

I. vii. Amidst preparations for a banquet in the King's honor, Macbeth and his wife discuss the murder. Macbeth's better nature fights against his ambition, but his wife plays on his masculine pride and steels him to proceed. Her plan is to ply the King's chamberlains with liquor until they are in a stupor and unable to interfere. She will contrive to make them appear guilty of the murder.

Entrance. **Sewer:** steward, butler.

1. **If it were done when 'tis done:** that is, if it would be done once and for all when it was done.

3. **trammel up:** confine in a net.

4. **his surcease:** Duncan's death; **that:** so that.

6. **But here:** on earth merely.

7. **jump the life to come:** overleap the question of eternity as though it were a minor obstacle.

11. **Commends:** offers; **ingredience:** ingredients composing the drink.

Lady. Your servants ever
Have theirs, themselves, and what is theirs, in compt,
To make their audit at your Highness' pleasure,
Still to return your own.

King. Give me your hand;
Conduct me to mine host. We love him highly
And shall continue our graces towards him.
By your leave, hostess.

Exeunt.

Scene VII. [The same. Macbeth's Castle.]

Hautboys. Torches. Enter a *Sewer*, and divers *Servants* with dishes and service over the stage. Then enter *Macbeth.*

Macb. If it were done when 'tis done, then 'twere well
It were done quickly. If the assassination
Could trammel up the consequence, and catch,
With his surcease, success, that but this blow
Might be the be-all and the end-all here,
But here, upon this bank and shoal of time,
We'ld jump the life to come. But in these cases
We still have judgment here, that we but teach
Bloody instructions, which, being taught, return
To plague the inventor. This even-handed justice
Commends the ingredience of our poisoned chalice
To our own lips. He's here in double trust:
First, as I am his kinsman and his subject,
Strong both against the deed; then, as his host,

17. **faculties:** powers.

18. **clear:** blameless, pure; see I. v. 80.

22. **Striding the blast:** straddling the wind as though on horseback; **cherubin:** members of the second order of angels.

23. **sightless:** invisible; see I. v. 53.

Who should against his murderer shut the door,
Not bear the knife myself. Besides, this Duncan
Hath borne his faculties so meek, hath been
So clear in his great office, that his virtues
Will plead like angels, trumpet-tongued, against
The deep damnation of his taking-off;
And pity, like a naked new-born babe,
Striding the blast, or heaven's cherubin, horsed
Upon the sightless couriers of the air,
Shall blow the horrid deed in every eye,
That tears shall drown the wind. I have no spur
To prick the sides of my intent, but only
Vaulting ambition, which o'erleaps itself
And falls on the other—

Enter *Lady* [*Macbeth*].

How now? What news?

Lady. He has almost supped. Why have you left the chamber?

Macb. Hath he asked for me?

Lady. Know you not he has?

Macb. We will proceed no further in this business.
He hath honored me of late, and I have bought
Golden opinions from all sorts of people,
Which would be worn now in their newest gloss,
Not cast aside so soon.

Lady. Was the hope drunk
Wherein you dressed yourself? Hath it slept since?
And wakes it now to look so green and pale
At what it did so freely? From this time

48. **wait upon:** follow in attendance, like a devoted servant.

49. **the poor cat i' the adage:** the cat who held back from catching fish for fear of wetting its feet.

52. **none:** that is, less than a man, an animal.

55. **durst:** dared.

59. **that their fitness:** their very fitness. Lady Macbeth indicates that Macbeth talked so bravely before only because he was not faced with an immediate opportunity to act and the fact that such an opportunity is now at hand has shaken him.

68. **But:** merely; see l. 6; **screw your courage to the sticking place:** that is, to its height. The image is probably from the mechanical devices used to tighten crossbows.

72. **wassail:** carouse, deep drinking; **convince:** conquer.

Such I account thy love. Art thou afeard
To be the same in thine own act and valor
As thou art in desire? Wouldst thou have that
Which thou esteem'st the ornament of life,
And live a coward in thine own esteem,
Letting "I dare not" wait upon "I would,"
Like the poor cat i' the adage?
Macb. Prithee peace!
I dare do all that may become a man.
Who dares do more is none.
Lady. What beast was't then
That made you break this enterprise to me?
When you durst do it, then you were a man;
And to be more than what you were, you would
Be so much more the man. Nor time nor place
Did then adhere, and yet you would make both.
They have made themselves, and that their fitness now
Does unmake you. I have given suck, and know
How tender 'tis to love the babe that milks me.
I would, while it was smiling in my face,
Have plucked my nipple from his boneless gums
And dashed the brains out, had I so sworn as you
Have done to this.
Macb. If we should fail?
Lady. We fail?
But screw your courage to the sticking place,
And we'll not fail. When Duncan is asleep
(Whereto the rather shall his day's hard journey
Soundly invite him), his two chamberlains
Will I with wine and wassail so convince
That memory, the warder of the brain,

74. **receipt:** container; that part of the brain which governs reason.

75. **limbeck:** alembic, or cap of the still which caught the fumes; i.e., merely a faint suggestion of itself.

78. **put upon:** impute to.

79. **spongy:** drink-sodden.

80. **quell:** killing.

82. **mettle:** spirit.

Shall be a fume, and the receipt of reason
A limbeck only. When in swinish sleep
Their drenched natures lie as in a death,
What cannot you and I perform upon
The unguarded Duncan? what not put upon
His spongy officers, who shall bear the guilt
Of our great quell?

Macb. Bring forth men-children only,
For thy undaunted mettle should compose
Nothing but males. Will it not be received,
When we have marked with blood those sleepy two
Of his own chamber and used their very daggers,
That they have done't?

Lady. Who dares receive it other,
As we shall make our griefs and clamor roar
Upon his death?

Macb. I am settled and bend up
Each corporal agent to this terrible feat.
Away, and mock the time with fairest show;
False face must hide what the false heart doth know.

Exeunt.

THE TRAGEDY OF

MACBETH

ACT II

II. i. Macbeth comes upon Banquo and his son Fleance as they are about to go to their beds. Banquo has been thinking of the prophecies, especially the prediction of rule for his children, and he broaches the subject to Macbeth. Macbeth pretends indifference but sounds out Banquo as a potential ally. Banquo makes it clear that he will not be a party to any dishonorable enterprise. After Banquo and his son have left him, Macbeth imagines he sees a dagger leading him to the King; hearing a bell, prearranged as a signal, he moves on to Duncan's chamber.

5. **husbandry:** thrifty management.

7. **Take thee that too:** Fleance has already taken his sword and Banquo now asks him to take his dagger as well. Many Elizabethan men went armed with both swords and daggers.

17. **largess:** tips; **offices:** the facilities for dispensing food and drink; that is, the servants who prepared and served Duncan's refreshment.

18. **withal:** with.

ACT II

Scene I. [The same. Court of Macbeth's Castle.]

Enter *Banquo,* and *Fleance* with a torch before him.

Ban. How goes the night, boy?
Fle. The moon is down; I have not heard the clock.
Ban. And she goes down at twelve.
Fle. I take't, 'tis later, sir.
Ban. Hold, take my sword. There's husbandry in heaven;
Their candles are all out. Take thee that too.
A heavy summons lies like lead upon me,
And yet I would not sleep. Merciful powers,
Restrain in me the cursed thoughts that nature
Gives way to in repose!

Enter *Macbeth,* and a *Servant* with a torch.

Give me my sword.
Who's there?
Macb. A friend.
Ban. What, sir, not yet at rest? The King's abed.
He hath been in unusual pleasure and
Sent forth great largess to your offices.
This diamond he greets your wife withal

19. **shut up:** concluded.

22. **Our will became the servant to defect:** our desire (to entertain Duncan lavishly) had to submit to our deficiencies.

32. **cleave to my consent:** ally yourself with me.

36. **franchised:** free, unbound by guilt.

37. **I shall be counseled:** I will be ready to listen to you.

45-6. **sensible/ To feeling:** i.e., tangible.

By the name of most kind hostess, and shut up
In measureless content.
Macb. Being unprepared,
Our will became the servant to defect,
Which else should free have wrought.
Ban. All's well.
I dreamt last night of the three Weird Sisters.
To you they have showed some truth.
Macb. I think not of them.
Yet when we can entreat an hour to serve,
We would spend it in some words upon that business,
If you would grant the time.
Ban. At your kind'st leisure.
Macb. If you shall cleave to my consent, when 'tis,
It shall make honor for you.
Ban. So I lose none
In seeking to augment it but still keep
My bosom franchised and allegiance clear,
I shall be counseled.
Macb. Good repose the while!
Ban. Thanks, sir. The like to you!
Exeunt Banquo [*and Fleance*].
Macb. Go bid thy mistress, when my drink is ready,
She strike upon the bell. Get thee to bed.
Exit [*Servant*].
Is this a dagger which I see before me,
The handle toward my hand? Come, let me clutch thee!
I have thee not, and yet I see thee still.
Art thou not, fatal vision, sensible
To feeling as to sight? or art thou but
A dagger of the mind, a false creation,

51. **marshal'st:** lead.

55. **dudgeon:** handle of a wood known as dudgeon.

57. **informs:** gives intelligence, reports.

59. **abuse:** deceive.

61. **Hecate:** the goddess who ruled magic and the dark doings of night.

64. **With Tarquin's ravishing strides:** Tarquin surprised and overcame the chaste Lucrece while she slept; this is the theme of Shakespeare's own poem "The Rape of Lucrece."

69. **Whiles:** while.

Proceeding from the heat-oppressed brain?
I see thee yet, in form as palpable
As this which now I draw.
Thou marshal'st me the way that I was going,
And such an instrument I was to use.
Mine eyes are made the fools o' the other senses,
Or else worth all the rest. I see thee still;
And on thy blade and dudgeon gouts of blood,
Which was not so before. There's no such thing.
It is the bloody business which informs
Thus to mine eyes. Now o'er the one half-world
Nature seems dead, and wicked dreams abuse
The curtained sleep. Witchcraft celebrates
Pale Hecate's offerings; and withered murder,
Alarumed by his sentinel, the wolf,
Whose howl's his watch, thus with his stealthy pace,
With Tarquin's ravishing strides, towards his design
Moves like a ghost. Thou sure and firm-set earth,
Hear not my steps which way they walk, for fear
Thy very stones prate of my whereabout
And take the present horror from the time,
Which now suits with it. Whiles I threat, he lives;
Words to the heat of deeds too cold breath gives.

A bell rings.

I go, and it is done. The bell invites me.
Hear it not, Duncan, for it is a knell
That summons thee to heaven, or to hell.

Exit.

II. ii. Lady Macbeth awaits her husband's return. She has seen to it that the chamberlains are drunk and drugged and has placed their daggers in convenient reach for Macbeth. Only Duncan's resemblance to her father prevented her from killing the King. Macbeth, the murder done, returns, dazed with horror. In his imagination he has heard a voice announcing that he has murdered sleep and will sleep no more. Terrified, he has brought his bloodstained weapons away with him. When Macbeth cannot summon the courage to return, Lady Macbeth takes the bloody daggers to incriminate the sleeping servants. A knocking is heard at the gate. Lady Macbeth urges her husband, who is still immobilized by his imagination, to go to bed lest they be found awake and arouse suspicion.

5. **the fatal bellman:** the town crier, who rang a bell as he made his rounds calling the time of night. At one time it was also his function to toll for the condemned man the night before execution.

8. **charge:** duty, their function of protecting the King.

9. **possets:** hot, spiced drinks, containing milk and laced with liquor.

15. **confounds:** destroys.

16. **he:** Duncan.

Scene II. [The same.]

Enter *Lady* [*Macbeth*].

Lady. That which hath made them drunk hath made me bold;
What hath quenched them hath given me fire. Hark! Peace!
It was the owl that shrieked, the fatal bellman
Which gives the stern'st good-night. He is about it.
The doors are open, and the surfeited grooms
Do mock their charge with snores. I have drugged their possets,
That death and nature do contend about them
Whether they live or die.

Macb. [*Within*] Who's there? What, ho?

Lady. Alack, I am afraid they have awaked,
And 'tis not done! The attempt, and not the deed,
Confounds us. Hark! I laid their daggers ready;
He could not miss 'em. Had he not resembled
My father as he slept, I had done't.

Enter *Macbeth*.

My husband!

Macb. I have done the deed. Didst thou not hear a noise?

Lady. I heard the owl scream and the crickets cry.
Did not you speak?

Macb. When?

Lady. Now.

30. **sorry:** deplorable.

32. **in's:** in his.

40. **hangman's hands:** the state executioner, besides performing the bloodless duty of hanging prisoners, was often called upon to hang, draw, and quarter traitors; a bloody business.

51. **raveled sleave:** tangled skein. **Sleave** means a skein of silk filaments.

53. **second course:** i.e., following food.

Macb. As I descended?
Lady. Ay.
Macb. Hark!
Who lies i' the second chamber?
Lady. Donalbain.
Macb. This is a sorry sight.
Lady. A foolish thought, to say a sorry sight.
Macb. There's one did laugh in's sleep, and one cried "Murder!"
That they did wake each other. I stood and heard them.
But they did say their prayers and addressed them
Again to sleep.
Lady. There are two lodged together.
Macb. One cried "God bless us!" and "Amen!" the other,
As they had seen me with these hangman's hands,
List'ning their fear. I could not say "Amen!"
When they did say "God bless us!"
Lady. Consider it not so deeply.
Macb. But wherefore could not I pronounce "Amen"?
I had most need of blessing, and "Amen"
Stuck in my throat.
Lady. These deeds must not be thought
After these ways. So, it will make us mad.
Macb. Methought I heard a voice cry "Sleep no more!
Macbeth does murder sleep"—the innocent sleep,
Sleep that knits up the raveled sleave of care,
The death of each day's life, sore labor's bath,
Balm of hurt minds, great nature's second course,
Chief nourisher in life's feast.
Lady. What do you mean?

62. **witness:** evidence.
80. **incarnadine:** redden.

Macb. Still it cried "Sleep no more!" to all the house;
"Glamis hath murdered sleep, and therefore Cawdor
Shall sleep no more! Macbeth shall sleep no more!"
Lady. Who was it that thus cried? Why, worthy Thane,
You do unbend your noble strength to think
So brainsickly of things. Go get some water
And wash this filthy witness from your hand.
Why did you bring these daggers from the place?
They must lie there. Go carry them and smear
The sleepy grooms with blood.
Macb. I'll go no more.
I am afraid to think what I have done;
Look on't again I dare not.
Lady. Infirm of purpose!
Give me the daggers. The sleeping and the dead
Are but as pictures. 'Tis the eye of childhood
That fears a painted devil. If he do bleed,
I'll gild the faces of the grooms withal,
For it must seem their guilt. *Exit. Knocking within.*
Macb. Whence is that knocking?
How is't with me when every noise appals me?
What hands are here? Ha! they pluck out mine eyes!
Will all great Neptune's ocean wash this blood
Clean from my hand? No. This my hand will rather
The multitudinous seas incarnadine,
Making the green one red.

Enter *Lady* [*Macbeth*].

Lady. My hands are of your color, but I shame
To wear a heart so white. *(Knock.)* I hear a knocking

86. **constancy:** composure.

88. **nightgown:** dressing gown.

89. **watchers:** wakers.

91. **To know my deed, 'twere best not know myself:** since full consciousness means realization of what I have done, it would be better if I could dull my faculties.

II. iii. The castle porter, reluctantly aroused from a drunken sleep, answers the gate, playing at being porter at hell's gate. He admits Lennox and Macduff, who are shortly greeted by their host. Macduff, directed to the King's chamber, quickly re-enters to announce the murder. Lennox and Macbeth go to view the scene and Macbeth kills the two grooms under pretense of rage at their murder of the King. Lady Macbeth faints, and the King's sons, Malcolm and Donalbain, slip away for safety, one to England, the other to Ireland.

---

2. **old:** a colloquialism for "plenty of."

4-5. **a farmer that hanged himself on the expectation of plenty:** i.e., because he feared overproduction and a low price for his crops.

5. **Come in time:** a welcoming expression; **napkins:** handkerchiefs; **enow:** enough.

8. **equivocator:** one who gives an answer which can be taken two ways, or which is limited by men-

[continued

12: see next page.

At the south entry. Retire we to our chamber.
A little water clears us of this deed.
How easy is it then! Your constancy
Hath left you unattended. *(Knock.)* Hark! more knocking.
Get on your nightgown, lest occasion call us
And show us to be watchers. Be not lost
So poorly in your thoughts.

Macb. To know my deed, 'twere best not know myself.
Knock.
Wake Duncan with thy knocking! I would thou couldst!
Exeunt.

Scene III. [The same.]

Enter a *Porter. Knocking within.*

Porter. Here's a knocking indeed! If a man were porter of hell gate, he should have old turning the key. *(Knock.)* Knock, knock, knock! Who's there, i' the name of Belzebub? Here's a farmer that hanged himself on the expectation of plenty. Come in time! Have napkins enow about you; here you'll sweat for't. *(Knock.)* Knock, knock! Who's there, in the other devil's name? Faith, here's an equivocator, that could swear in both the scales against either scale; who committed treason enough for God's sake, yet could not equivocate to heaven. O, come in, equivocator! *(Knock.)* Knock, knock, knock! Who's there? Faith, here's an English tailor come hither for stealing

tal reservations. This practice was charged against Jesuits, whose loyalty to the English crown was suspect, and this passage has been regarded as an allusion to the Jesuit priest Father Garnet, who was implicated in the Gunpowder Plot and executed in 1606.

12-3. **stealing out of a French hose: French hose** were breeches. Dishonest tailors often skimped on garments and kept the excess from the material supplied by the customer for their own use.

14. **goose:** the iron used for pressing his handiwork.

26. **nose-painting:** reddening of the nose common in habitual drinkers.

35. **on:** of.

35-6. **requited:** repaid.

37. **took up my legs:** the porter pictures drink as wrestling with him.

37-8. **made a shift:** managed.

out of a French hose. Come in, tailor. Here you may roast your goose. *(Knock.)* Knock, knock! Never at quiet! What are you? But this place is too cold for hell. I'll devil-porter it no further. I had thought to have let in some of all professions that go the primrose way to the everlasting bonfire. *(Knock.)* Anon, anon! [*Opens the gate.*] I pray you remember the porter.

Enter *Macduff* and *Lennox.*

Macd. Was it so late, friend, ere you went to bed, That you do lie so late?

Port. Faith, sir, we were carousing till the second cock; and drink, sir, is a great provoker of three things.

Macd. What three things does drink especially provoke?

Port. Marry, sir, nose-painting, sleep, and urine. Lechery, sir, it provokes, and unprovokes: it provokes the desire, but it takes away the performance. Therefore much drink may be said to be an equivocator with lechery: it makes him, and it mars him; it sets him on, and it takes him off; it persuades him, and disheartens him; makes him stand to, and not stand to; in conclusion, equivocates him in a sleep, and, giving him the lie, leaves him.

Macd. I believe drink gave thee the lie last night.

Port. That it did, sir, i' the very throat on me; but I requited him for his lie; and, I think, being too strong for him, though he took up my legs sometime, yet I made a shift to cast him.

Macd. Is thy master stirring?

50. **physics:** remedies. **Physic** was a general term for medicine.

53. **limited:** appointed.

60. **combustion:** uproar.

61. **The obscure bird:** the owl. **Obscure** is used in the sense of "dark," the owl being nocturnal.

Enter *Macbeth.*

Our knocking has awaked him; here he comes.
Len. Good morrow, noble sir.
Macb. Good morrow, both.
Macd. Is the King stirring, worthy Thane?
Macb. Not yet.
Macd. He did command me to call timely on him;
I have almost slipped the hour.
Macb. I'll bring you to him.
Macd. I know this is a joyful trouble to you;
But yet 'tis one.
Macb. The labor we delight in physics pain.
This is the door.
Macd. I'll make so bold to call,
For 'tis my limited service. *Exit.*
Len. Goes the King hence today?
Macb. He does; he did appoint so.
Len. The night has been unruly. Where we lay,
Our chimneys were blown down; and, as they say,
Lamentings heard i' the air, strange screams of death,
And prophesying, with accents terrible,
Of dire combustion and confused events
New hatched to the woeful time. The obscure bird
Clamored the livelong night. Some say the earth
Was feverous and did shake.
Macb. 'Twas a rough night.
Len. My young remembrance cannot parallel
A fellow to it.

70. **Confusion:** destruction; see **confounds,** II. ii. 15.

72. **The Lord's anointed temple:** i.e., the King's body.

77. **Gorgon:** the mythological monster also known as Medusa, who petrified anyone who gazed upon her face.

84. **The great doom's image:** a likeness of Judgment Day.

85-6. **like sprites/ To countenance this horror:** like spirits, in keeping with the scene, which resembles the Day of Judgment.

Enter *Macduff.*

Macd. O horror, horror, horror! Tongue nor heart
Cannot conceive nor name thee!
Macb. and Len. What's the matter?
Macd. Confusion now hath made his masterpiece!
Most sacrilegious murder hath broke ope
The Lord's anointed temple and stole thence
The life o' the building!
Macb. What is't you say? the life?
Len. Mean you his Majesty?
Macd. Approach the chamber, and destroy your sight
With a new Gorgon. Do not bid me speak.
See, and then speak yourselves.
Exeunt Macbeth and Lennox.
Awake, awake!
Ring the alarum bell. Murder and treason!
Banquo and Donalbain! Malcolm! awake!
Shake off this downy sleep, death's counterfeit,
And look on death itself! Up, up, and see
The great doom's image! Malcolm! Banquo!
As from your graves rise up and walk like sprites
To countenance this horror! Ring the bell!
Bell rings.

Enter *Lady* [*Macbeth*].

Lady. What's the business,
That such a hideous trumpet calls to parley
The sleepers of the house? Speak, speak!

103. **mortality:** human life.
104. **toys:** trifles; **grace:** honor; see I. iii. 60.
105. **drawn:** drawn off; that is, used up.

Macd. O gentle lady,
'Tis not for you to hear what I can speak!
The repetition in a woman's ear
Would murder as it fell.

Enter *Banquo.*

O Banquo, Banquo,
Our royal master's murdered!
Lady. Woe, alas!
What, in our house?
Ban. Too cruel anywhere.
Dear Duff, I prithee contradict thyself
And say it is not so.

Enter *Macbeth, Lennox,* and *Ross.*

Macb. Had I but died an hour before this chance,
I had lived a blessed time; for from this instant
There's nothing serious in mortality;
All is but toys; renown and grace is dead;
The wine of life is drawn, and the mere lees
Is left this vault to brag of.

Enter *Malcolm* and *Donalbain.*

Don. What is amiss?
Macb. You are, and do not know't.
The spring, the head, the fountain of your blood
Is stopped, the very source of it is stopped.
Macd. Your royal father's murdered.

114. **badged:** marked, as with a badge.

122. **amazed:** numb in mind from shock.

125. **expedition:** speed.

128. **breach:** break in its defenses.

131. **Unmannerly breeched with gore:** that is, their nakedness covered with blood instead of proper sheaths.

133. **make's:** make his.

138. **argument:** topic of discussion.

140. **hid in an auger hole:** concealed where we would not look for it.

Mal. O, by whom?
Len. Those of his chamber, as it seemed, had done't.
Their hands and faces were all badged with blood;
So were their daggers, which unwiped we found
Upon their pillows.
They stared and were distracted. No man's life
Was to be trusted with them.
Macb. O, yet I do repent me of my fury
That I did kill them.
Macd. Wherefore did you so?
Macb. Who can be wise, amazed, temp'rate, and furious,
Loyal and neutral, in a moment? No man.
The expedition of my violent love
Outrun the pauser, reason. Here lay Duncan,
His silver skin laced with his golden blood,
And his gashed stabs looked like a breach in nature
For ruin's wasteful entrance; there, the murderers,
Steeped in the colors of their trade, their daggers
Unmannerly breeched with gore. Who could refrain
That had a heart to love and in that heart
Courage to make's love known?
Lady. Help me hence, ho!
Macd. Look to the lady.
Mal. [*Aside to Donalbain*] Why do we hold our tongues,
That most may claim this argument for ours?
Don. [*Aside to Malcolm*] What should be spoken here,
Where our fate, hid in an auger hole,
May rush and seize us? Let's away,
Our tears are not yet brewed.

149. **scruples:** doubts.

151. **pretense:** intention, purpose.

155. **briefly:** speedily, without delay.

161-62. **Our separated fortune/ Shall keep us both the safer:** that is, we shall be safer if we go our separate ways.

163-64. **the near in blood,/ The nearer bloody:** The nearer we are related to a man, the nearer we are to his violence.

168. **dainty of:** particular about.

169. **shift:** sneak.

169-70. **that theft/ Which steals itself when there's no mercy left:** the theft of themselves from a situation which promises no mercy.

Mal. [*Aside to Donalbain*] Nor our strong sorrow
Upon the foot of motion.
Ban. Look to the lady.
[*Lady Macbeth is carried out.*]
And when we have our naked frailties hid,
That suffer in exposure, let us meet
And question this most bloody piece of work,
To know it further. Fears and scruples shake us.
In the great hand of God I stand, and thence
Against the undivulged pretense I fight
Of treasonous malice.
Macd. And so do I.
All. So all.
Macb. Let's briefly put on manly readiness
And meet i' the hall together.
All. Well contented.
Exeunt [*all but Malcolm and Donalbain*].
Mal. What will you do? Let's not consort with them.
To show an unfelt sorrow is an office
Which the false man does easy. I'll to England.
Don. To Ireland I. Our separated fortune
Shall keep us both the safer. Where we are,
There's daggers in men's smiles; the near in blood,
The nearer bloody.
Mal. This murderous shaft that's shot
Hath not yet lighted, and our safest way
Is to avoid the aim. Therefore to horse!
And let us not be dainty of leave-taking
But shift away. There's warrant in that theft
Which steals itself when there's no mercy left.
Exeunt.

II. iv. Ross and an old man discuss the unnatural happenings of recent hours. Macduff reports the rumor that because of their flight Malcolm and Donalbain are accused of complicity in their father's death. Macbeth has already been named King and has gone to be crowned at Scone. Ross plans to attend the coronation, but Macduff refuses to go, showing uneasiness at Macbeth's accession.

---

3. **sore:** grievous, terrible.

4. **Hath trifled:** has made trifles of (by comparison).

6. **As:** as if.

8. **the traveling lamp:** i.e., the sun.

9. **Is't night's predominance, or the day's shame:** is it because of night's greater power or day's shame to show her face.

14. **tow'ring in her pride of place:** proudly soaring to the greatest height she can achieve.

18. **minions:** darlings; that is, the pick of their kind; see I. ii. 21.

20. **as:** as if; see l. 6.

Scene IV. [The same. Without Macbeth's Castle.]

Enter *Ross* with an *Old Man.*

Old Man. Threescore and ten I can remember well;
Within the volume of which time I have seen
Hours dreadful and things strange; but this sore night
Hath trifled former knowings.

Ross. Ah, good father,
Thou seest the heavens, as troubled with man's act,
Threaten his bloody stage. By the clock 'tis day,
And yet dark night strangles the traveling lamp.
Is't night's predominance, or the day's shame,
That darkness does the face of earth entomb
When living light should kiss it?

Old Man. 'Tis unnatural,
Even like the deed that's done. On Tuesday last
A falcon, tow'ring in her pride of place,
Was by a mousing owl hawked at and killed.

Ross. And Duncan's horses (a thing most strange and certain),
Beauteous and swift, the minions of their race,
Turned wild in nature, broke their stalls, flung out,
Contending 'gainst obedience, as they would make
War with mankind.

Old Man. 'Tis said they eat each other.

Ross. They did so, to the amazement of mine eyes
That looked upon't.

Enter *Macduff*.

31. **pretend:** intend; see II. iii. 151.

32. **suborned:** hired or otherwise persuaded.

36. **'Gainst nature still:** i.e., another unnatural act.

37. **raven up:** snap up greedily.

40. **Scone:** the traditional site of the crowning of Scottish kings. Edward I, known as "the hammer of the Scots," seized the Stone of Scone, the coronation seat, and took it to England, where it can still be seen in Westminster Abbey.

43. **Colmekill:** the modern island of Iona; the former site of one of Saint Columba's monasteries.

49. **may you see things well done there:** that is, Macduff is uneasy about the outcome of Macbeth's accession to the throne.

51. **Lest our old robes sit easier than our new:** a continuation of his expression of uneasiness; Macbeth's rule may be harsher than that of Duncan.

53. **benison:** blessing.

Macbeth's coronation.
From Holinshed, *The Historie of Scotland . . .* (1577).

Here comes the good Macduff.
How goes the world, sir, now?

Macd. Why, see you not?

Ross. Is't known who did this more than bloody deed?

Macd. Those that Macbeth hath slain.

Ross. Alas, the day!
What good could they pretend?

Macd. They were suborned.
Malcolm and Donalbain, the King's two sons,
Are stol'n away and fled, which puts upon them
Suspicion of the deed.

Ross. 'Gainst nature still!
Thriftless ambition, that will raven up
Thine own live's means! Then 'tis most like
The sovereignty will fall upon Macbeth.

Macd. He is already named, and gone to Scone
To be invested.

Ross. Where is Duncan's body?

Macd. Carried to Colmekill,
The sacred storehouse of his predecessors
And guardian of their bones.

Ross. Will you to Scone?

Macd. No, cousin, I'll to Fife.

Ross. Well, I will thither.

Macd. Well, may you see things well done there. Adieu,
Lest our old robes sit easier than our new!

Ross. Farewell, father.

Old Man. God's benison go with you, and with those
That would make good of bad, and friends of foes!

Exeunt omnes.

THE TRAGEDY OF

MACBETH

ACT III

III. i. Banquo suspects Macbeth's guilt. Macbeth urges his presence at a banquet but Banquo is about to ride forth and does not promise to return in time. He evades Macbeth's questions, but Macbeth establishes that Fleance will accompany him. Macbeth persuades two malcontents that Banquo is their enemy and exacts their promise to kill him and Fleance before they return that night. He hates Banquo because of the prediction that Banquo's children will rule in Scotland and no child of his own will succeed him.

---

4. **stand:** continue.

8. **on thee made good:** proved in your case.

S.D. after l. 10. **Sennet:** trumpet sequence to announce the arrival of important persons.

14. **all-thing:** altogether.

15. **solemn:** formal.

ACT III

Scene I. [Forres. The Palace.]

Enter *Banquo*.

Ban. Thou hast it now–King, Cawdor, Glamis, all,
As the Weird Women promised; and I fear
Thou play'dst most foully for't. Yet it was said
It should not stand in thy posterity,
But that myself should be the root and father
Of many kings. If there come truth from them
(As upon thee, Macbeth, their speeches shine),
Why, by the verities on thee made good,
May they not be my oracles as well
And set me up in hope? But, hush, no more!

Sennet sounded. Enter *Macbeth*, as *King; Lady* [*Macbeth*, as *Queen*]; *Lennox, Ross, Lords*, and *Attendants*.

Macb. Here's our chief guest.
Lady. If he had been forgotten,
It had been as a gap in our great feast,
And all-thing unbecoming.
Macb. Tonight we hold a solemn supper, sir,
And I'll request your presence.
Ban. Let your Highness

24. **grave and prosperous:** deeply considered and profitable.

37. **cause of state:** state affairs.

40. **Our time does call upon's:** the shortness of time urges us to depart.

46. **ourself:** i.e., myself; the royal plural.

Command upon me, to the which my duties
Are with a most indissoluble tie
For ever knit.
Macb. Ride you this afternoon?
Ban. Ay, my good lord.
Macb. We should have else desired your good advice
(Which still hath been both grave and prosperous)
In this day's council; but we'll take tomorrow.
Is't far you ride?
Ban. As far, my lord, as will fill up the time
'Twixt this and supper. Go not my horse the better,
I must become a borrower of the night
For a dark hour or twain.
Macb. Fail not our feast.
Ban. My lord, I will not.
Macb. We hear our bloody cousins are bestowed
In England and in Ireland, not confessing
Their cruel parricide, filling their hearers
With strange invention. But of that tomorrow,
When therewithal we shall have cause of state
Craving us jointly. Hie you to horse. Adieu,
Till you return at night. Goes Fleance with you?
Ban. Ay, my good lord. Our time does call upon's.
Macb. I wish your horses swift and sure of foot,
And so I do commend you to their backs.
Farewell.

Exit Banquo.

Let every man be master of his time
Till seven at night. To make society
The sweeter welcome, we will keep ourself

Frontispiece of *News from Scotland* (1591), a tract about the activities of Scottish witches, from which Shakespeare may have derived material for his witches.

47. **While then:** in the meantime.
48. **Attend:** that is, are they awaiting.
52. **To be thus:** to have achieved the throne.
55. **would:** should, must.
60. **genius:** the ruling spirit of his nature.
69. **filed:** defiled.
72. **eternal jewel:** soul.
73. **the common enemy of man:** the devil.

Till supper time alone. While then, God be with you!
Exeunt Lords [and others. Manent Macbeth and a Servant].
Sirrah, a word with you. Attend those men
Our pleasure?
Serv. They are, my lord, without the palace gate.
Macb. Bring them before us. *Exit Servant.*
To be thus is nothing,
But to be safely thus. Our fears in Banquo
Stick deep, and in his royalty of nature
Reigns that which would be feared. 'Tis much he dares,
And to that dauntless temper of his mind
He hath a wisdom that doth guide his valor
To act in safety. There is none but he
Whose being I do fear; and under him
My genius is rebuked, as it is said
Mark Antony's was by Cæsar. He chid the Sisters
When first they put the name of King upon me,
And bade them speak to him. Then, prophet-like,
They hailed him father to a line of kings.
Upon my head they placed a fruitless crown
And put a barren scepter in my gripe,
Thence to be wrenched with an unlineal hand,
No son of mine succeeding. If't be so,
For Banquo's issue have I filed my mind;
For them the gracious Duncan have I murdered;
Put rancors in the vessel of my peace
Only for them, and mine eternal jewel
Given to the common enemy of man
To make them kings, the seed of Banquo kings!

75. **list:** lists; that is, the field of combat.

76. **champion me to the utterance:** like a champion of chivalry engage me *à l'outrance* (to the death).

84. **made good:** proved; see l. 8.

85. **passed in probation:** examined and proved.

86. **borne in hand:** deceived, "strung along."

89. **notion:** understanding.

95. **gospeled:** ruled by the gospels as to forbearance of injury.

Rather than so, come, Fate, into the list,
And champion me to the utterance! Who's there?

Enter *Servant* and two *Murderers.*

Now go to the door and stay there till we call.
Exit Servant.

Was it not yesterday we spoke together?
Murderers. It was, so please your Highness.
Macb. Well then, now
Have you considered of my speeches? Know
That it was he, in the times past, which held you
So under fortune, which you thought had been
Our innocent self. This I made good to you
In our last conference, passed in probation with you
How you were borne in hand, how crossed; the instruments;
Who wrought with them; and all things else that might
To half a soul and to a notion crazed
Say "Thus did Banquo."
1. Mur. You made it known to us.
Macb. I did so; and went further, which is now
Our point of second meeting. Do you find
Your patience so predominant in your nature
That you can let this go? Are you so gospeled
To pray for this good man and for his issue,
Whose heavy hand hath bowed you to the grave
And beggared yours for ever?
1. Mur. We are men, my liege.
Macb. Ay, in the catalogue ye go for men,

102. **Shoughs, water-rugs:** two kinds of dogs; **clept:** called.

103. **valued file:** list which includes an appraisal of worth.

108. **Particular addition:** a distinguishing title; see I. iii. 113.

116. **were:** would be.

123. **set:** stake.

124. **on't:** of it.

128. **in such bloody distance:** so opposed in hostility.

129-30. **thrusts/ Against:** physically threatens; **near'st of life:** heart; very existence.

As hounds and greyhounds, mongrels, spaniels, curs,
Shoughs, water-rugs, and demi-wolves are clept
All by the name of dogs. The valued file
Distinguishes the swift, the slow, the subtle,
The housekeeper, the hunter, every one
According to the gift which bounteous nature
Hath in him closed; whereby he does receive
Particular addition, from the bill
That writes them all alike; and so of men.
Now, if you have a station in the file,
Not i' the worst rank of manhood, say't;
And I will put that business in your bosoms
Whose execution takes your enemy off,
Grapples you to the heart and love of us,
Who wear our health but sickly in his life,
Which in his death were perfect.

2. Mur. I am one, my liege,
Whom the vile blows and buffets of the world
Have so incensed that I am reckless what
I do to spite the world.

1. Mur. And I another,
So weary with disasters, tugged with fortune,
That I would set my life on any chance,
To mend it or be rid on't.

Macb. Both of you
Know Banquo was your enemy.

Murderers. True, my lord.

Macb. So is he mine, and in such bloody distance
That every minute of his being thrusts
Against my near'st of life; and though I could

132. **bid my will avouch it:** justify it as my will, as a tyrant might.

134. **but wail:** "must" has to be understood here: **I may not drop, but** [I must] **wail.**

145. **the perfect spy:** the most accurate report available.

147. **something:** somewhat away; **always thought:** remembering always.

148. **clearness:** freedom from implication.

149. **rubs:** imperfections.

153. **Resolve yourselves apart:** withdraw and decide.

156. **straight:** immediately.

157. **concluded:** agreed upon.

The murder of Banquo.

From Holinshed, *The Historie of Scotland* . . . (1577).

With barefaced power sweep him from my sight
And bid my will avouch it, yet I must not,
For certain friends that are both his and mine,
Whose loves I may not drop, but wail his fall
Who I myself struck down. And thence it is
That I to your assistance do make love,
Masking the business from the common eye
For sundry weighty reasons.

2. Mur. We shall, my lord,
Perform what you command us.

1. Mur. Though our lives—

Macb. Your spirits shine through you. Within this hour at most
I will advise you where to plant yourselves,
Acquaint you with the perfect spy o' the time,
The moment on't; for't must be done tonight,
And something from the palace (always thought
That I require a clearness), and with him,
To leave no rubs nor botches in the work,
Fleance his son, that keeps him company,
Whose absence is no less material to me
Than is his father's, must embrace the fate
Of that dark hour. Resolve yourselves apart;
I'll come to you anon.

Murderers. We are resolved, my lord.

Macb. I'll call upon you straight. Abide within.

[*Exeunt Murderers.*]

It is concluded. Banquo, thy soul's flight,
If it find heaven, must find it out tonight.

Exit.

III. ii. Lady Macbeth, now Queen, finds her position less happy than she had expected, but she attempts to encourage her husband, who confides to her something of his own torment. He urges her to be particularly attentive to Banquo at the evening's feast, and, though he hints at a dreadful deed to be done that night, does not tell her of his plan to kill Banquo and Fleance.

11. **sorriest:** most wretched.

13. **without:** beyond.

15. **scotched:** cut or damaged so as to be harmless. The Folio has "scorch'd" which has much the same meaning and was derived from "score."

16. **close:** heal.

18. **the frame of things disjoint:** the framework of the universe come apart.

23. **torture:** i.e., rack.

24. **In restless ecstasy:** tossing sleeplessly from mental conflict.

Scene II. [The same.]

Enter *Macbeth's Lady* and a *Servant.*

Lady. Is Banquo gone from court?
Serv. Ay, madam, but returns again tonight.
Lady. Say to the King I would attend his leisure
For a few words.
Serv. Madam, I will. *Exit.*
Lady. Naught's had, all's spent,
Where our desire is got without content.
'Tis safer to be that which we destroy
Than by destruction dwell in doubtful joy.

Enter *Macbeth.*

How now, my lord? Why do you keep alone,
Of sorriest fancies your companions making,
Using those thoughts which should indeed have died
With them they think on? Things without all remedy
Should be without regard. What's done is done.
Macb. We have scotched the snake, not killed it.
She'll close and be herself, whilst our poor malice
Remains in danger of her former tooth.
But let the frame of things disjoint, both the worlds suffer,
Ere we will eat our meal in fear and sleep
In the affliction of these terrible dreams
That shake us nightly. Better be with the dead,
Whom we, to gain our peace, have sent to peace,
Than on the torture of the mind to lie
In restless ecstasy. Duncan is in his grave;

25. **fitful:** irregular.

27. **malice domestic:** rebellion; **foreign levy:** foreign troops.

34. **Present him eminence:** single him out for special attention.

35. **Unsafe the while:** that is, we are unsafe so long as we must, etc.; the necessity of courting Banquo is an indication of their precarious position.

36. **lave:** wash.

37. **vizards:** masks.

42. **Nature's copy's not eterne:** that is, they have not been granted eternal life. Many editors believe that **copy** refers to copyhold tenure, which permitted a tenant to hold land at the will of the lord of the manor, an impermanent lease. Whether Shakespeare had this in mind is impossible to determine but the ultimate meaning of the passage is clear enough.

45. **cloistered:** i.e., by the confined places in which he habitually flies—deserted buildings, belfries, etc.

46. **shard-borne:** borne on wings like shards (pieces of pottery).

50. **chuck:** i.e., chick.

51. **seeling:** blinding, in falconry the process of sewing the eyelids of a bird to tame it.

52. **Scarf up:** cover with a scarf; blindfold.

54. **that great bond:** the promise of the Weird Sisters that Banquo's descendants will rule instead of Macbeth's heirs.

After life's fitful fever he sleeps well.
Treason has done his worst: nor steel nor poison,
Malice domestic, foreign levy, nothing,
Can touch him further.
Lady. Come on.
Gentle my lord, sleek o'er your rugged looks;
Be bright and jovial among your guests tonight.
Macb. So shall I, love; and so, I pray, be you.
Let your remembrance apply to Banquo;
Present him eminence both with eye and tongue:
Unsafe the while, that we
Must lave our honors in these flattering streams
And make our faces vizards to our hearts,
Disguising what they are.
Lady. You must leave this.
Macb. O, full of scorpions is my mind, dear wife!
Thou know'st that Banquo, and his Fleance, lives.
Lady. But in them Nature's copy's not eterne.
Macb. There's comfort yet; they are assailable.
Then be thou jocund. Ere the bat hath flown
His cloistered flight, ere to black Hecate's summons
The shard-borne beetle with his drowsy hums
Hath rung night's yawning peal, there shall be done
A deed of dreadful note.
Lady. What's to be done?
Macb. Be innocent of the knowledge, dearest chuck,
Till thou applaud the deed. Come, seeling night,
Scarf up the tender eye of pitiful day,
And with thy bloody and invisible hand
Cancel and tear to pieces that great bond

56. **the rooky wood:** the wood is filled with other crows (rooks) and is **rooky** (gloomy). Shakespeare very likely had both meanings of the word in mind.

III. iii. Macbeth's assassins, joined by a third man, ambush Banquo and Fleance. Banquo is killed but Fleance escapes in the dark.

---

4. **offices:** duties.

5. **To the direction just:** that is, exactly as Macbeth has already directed.

8. **lated:** belated; **apace:** speedily.

9. **To gain the timely inn:** to reach an inn in time (before dark).

14. **within the note of expectation:** on the list of guests expected.

16. **His horses go about:** servants have taken the horses to be put up for the night.

Which keeps me pale! Light thickens, and the crow
Makes wing to the rooky wood.
Good things of day begin to droop and drowse,
Whiles night's black agents to their preys do rouse.
Thou marvell'st at my words; but hold thee still:
Things bad begun make strong themselves by ill.
So prithee go with me.

Exeunt.

Scene III. [The same. A park near the Palace.]

Enter three *Murderers.*

1. Mur. But who did bid thee join with us?
3. Mur. Macbeth.
2. Mur. He needs not our mistrust, since he delivers
Our offices, and what we have to do,
To the direction just.
1. Mur. Then stand with us.
The west yet glimmers with some streaks of day.
Now spurs the lated traveler apace
To gain the timely inn, and near approaches
The subject of our watch.
3. Mur. Hark! I hear horses.
Ban. (Within) Give us a light there, ho!
2. Mur. Then 'tis he! The rest
That are within the note of expectation
Already are i' the court.
1. Mur. His horses go about.
3. Mur. Almost a mile; but he does usually,

III. iv. As Macbeth presides at the banquet, one of the assassins reports. Macbeth is shaken by Fleance's escape but is assured that Banquo is safely dead. Recalled by his wife to his duties as host, he is toasting the company and the absent Banquo when he sees the latter's bloody ghost, invisible to all but himself. Lady Macbeth tries to pass off his suspicious behavior as a recurring affliction, but Macbeth is so completely unmanned by the apparition that she is forced to dismiss the guests. Alone with his wife, Macbeth tells her that Macduff is virtually in revolt. He plans to consult the three witches the next day and hints at further bloody deeds.

1. **your own degrees:** where your rank entitles you to sit.

1-2. **At first/ And last:** to all in whatever degree.

So all men do, from hence to the palace gate
Make it their walk.

Enter *Banquo*, and *Fleance* with a torch.

2. *Mur.* A light, a light!
3. *Mur.* 'Tis he.
1. *Mur.* Stand to't.
Ban. It will be rain tonight.
1. *Mur.* Let it come down!
[*They set upon Banquo.*]
Ban. O, treachery! Fly, good Fleance, fly, fly, fly!
Thou mayst revenge. O slave!
[*Dies. Fleance escapes.*]
3. *Mur.* Who did strike out the light?
1. *Mur.* Was't not the way?
3. *Mur.* There's but one down; the son is fled.
2. *Mur.* We have lost
Best half of our affair.
1. *Mur.* Well, let's away, and say how much is done.
Exeunt.

Scene IV. [The same. Hall in the Palace.]

Banquet prepared. Enter *Macbeth*, *Lady* [*Macbeth*], *Ross*, *Lennox*, *Lords*, and *Attendants*.

Macb. You know your own degrees, sit down. At first
And last the hearty welcome.
Lords. Thanks to your Majesty.

6. **keeps her state:** retains her dignity (by sitting in her chair of state instead of at table with the guests); **in best time:** at the appropriate time.

7. **require:** ask as a favor, not demand.

10. **encounter:** meet; that is, respond to.

13. **large:** great; that is, enjoy yourselves heartily.

28. **founded:** rooted, stable.

29. **broad and general:** free and unlimited (in spirit); **casing:** enveloping, surrounding everything.

31. **safe:** i.e., no longer to be feared.

Macb. Ourself will mingle with society
And play the humble host.
Our hostess keeps her state, but in best time
We will require her welcome.
Lady. Pronounce it for me, sir, to all our friends,
For my heart speaks they are welcome.

Enter *First Murderer* [to the door].

Macb. See, they encounter thee with their hearts' thanks.
Both sides are even: here I'll sit i' the midst.
Be large in mirth; anon we'll drink a measure
The table round. [*Moves toward Murderer at door.*]
There's blood upon thy face.
Mur. 'Tis Banquo's then.
Macb. 'Tis better thee without than he within.
Is he dispatched?
Mur. My lord, his throat is cut. That I did for him.
Macb. Thou art the best o' the cutthroats! Yet he's good
That did the like for Fleance. If thou didst it,
Thou art the nonpareil.
Mur. Most royal sir,
Fleance is scaped.
Macb. [*Aside*] Then comes my fit again. I had else been perfect;
Whole as the marble, founded as the rock,
As broad and general as the casing air.
But now I am cabined, cribbed, confined, bound in
To saucy doubts and fears.—But Banquo's safe?
Mur. Ay, my good lord. Safe in a ditch he bides,

36. **worm:** serpent; that is, Fleance.

39. **hear ourselves:** speak together.

41. **give the cheer:** offer spontaneous hospitality.

41-3. **The feast is sold/ That is not often vouched, while 'tis a-making,/ 'Tis given with welcome:** a feast is like buying a meal in an inn unless the host keeps his guests assured of their welcome.

43. **To feed:** eating merely to feed the body; **were:** would be.

44. **thence:** i.e., home; **ceremony:** courteous formality.

50. **our country's honor, roofed:** those who best represent Scotland's honor under one roof.

51. **graced:** honored; see II. iii. 104.

52-3. **Who may I rather challenge for unkindness/ Than pity for mischance:** whose absence, I hope, may be laid to an unkind refusal to come rather than to an accident which prevents his presence.

With twenty trenched gashes on his head,
The least a death to nature.
Macb. Thanks for that!
There the grown serpent lies; the worm that's fled
Hath nature that in time will venom breed,
No teeth for the present. Get thee gone. Tomorrow
We'll hear ourselves again.
Exit Murderer.
Lady. My royal lord,
You do not give the cheer. The feast is sold
That is not often vouched, while 'tis a-making,
'Tis given with welcome. To feed were best at home.
From thence, the sauce to meat is ceremony;
Meeting were bare without it.

Enter the *Ghost of Banquo,* and sits in *Macbeth's* place.

Macb. Sweet remembrancer!
Now good digestion wait on appetite,
And health on both!
Len. May't please your Highness sit.
Macb. Here had we now our country's honor, roofed,
Were the graced person of our Banquo present;
Who may I rather challenge for unkindness
Than pity for mischance!
Ross. His absence, sir,
Lays blame upon his promise. Please't your Highness
To grace us with your royal company?
Macb. The table's full.
Len. Here is a place reserved, sir.
Macb. Where?

69. **upon a thought:** in a moment.

71. **passion:** fit.

77. **air-drawn:** created by, and insubstantial as, air.

78. **flaws:** storms of emotion.

79. **Impostors to true fear:** a case of nerves rather than genuine fear.

87. **charnel houses:** repositories of human bones in cemeteries.

88-9. **our monuments/ Shall be the maws of kites:** that is, our bodies will be thrown to scavengers instead of being buried. **Maw** means stomach.

Len. Here, my good lord. What is't that moves your Highness?
Macb. Which of you have done this?
Lords. What, my good lord?
Macb. Thou canst not say I did it. Never shake
Thy gory locks at me.
Ross. Gentlemen, rise. His Highness is not well.
Lady. Sit, worthy friends. My lord is often thus,
And hath been from his youth. Pray you keep seat.
The fit is momentary; upon a thought
He will again be well. If much you note him,
You shall offend him and extend his passion.
Feed, and regard him not.—Are you a man?
Macb. Ay, and a bold one, that dare look on that
Which might appal the devil.
Lady. O proper stuff!
This is the very painting of your fear.
This is the air-drawn dagger which you said
Led you to Duncan. O, these flaws and starts
(Impostors to true fear) would well become
A woman's story at a winter's fire,
Authorized by her grandam. Shame itself!
Why do you make such faces? When all's done,
You look but on a stool.
Macb. Prithee see there! behold! look! lo! How say you?
Why, what care I? If thou canst nod, speak too.
If charnel houses and our graves must send
Those that we bury back, our monuments
Shall be the maws of kites.

[*Exit Ghost.*]

94. **purged the gentle weal:** purged society of violence and tamed it.

99. **mortal murders:** fatal wounds; see I. v. 45.

111-12. **To all, and him, we thirst,/ And all to all:** I am eager to toast everyone, especially Banquo, and let all drink to all.

113. **Our duties, and the pledge:** we avow our allegiance and drink the good health of all.

114. **Avaunt:** get hence.

Lady. What, quite unmanned in folly?
Macb. If I stand here, I saw him.
Lady. Fie, for shame!
Macb. Blood hath been shed ere now, i' the olden time,
Ere humane statute purged the gentle weal;
Ay, and since too, murders have been performed
Too terrible for the ear. The time has been
That, when the brains were out, the man would die,
And there an end! But now they rise again,
With twenty mortal murders on their crowns,
And push us from our stools. This is more strange
Than such a murder is.
Lady. My worthy lord,
Your noble friends do lack you.
Macb. I do forget.
Do not muse at me, my most worthy friends.
I have a strange infirmity, which is nothing
To those that know me. Come, love and health to all!
Then I'll sit down. Give me some wine, fill full.

Enter *Ghost.*

I drink to the general joy o' the whole table,
And to our dear friend Banquo, whom we miss.
Would he were here! To all, and him, we thirst,
And all to all.
Lords. Our duties, and the pledge.
Macb. Avaunt, and quit my sight! Let the earth hide thee!
Thy bones are marrowless, thy blood is cold;

117. **speculation:** discernment; ability to see and report to the brain.

124. **Hyrcan:** Hyrcania was a desert area near the Caspian Sea.

127. **dare me to the desert:** challenge me to a fight without quarter in a solitary place where there will be no hope of help.

128. **inhabit:** abide, bide at home; refuse to meet your challenge.

135. **admired:** amazing.

137. **overcome us like a summer's cloud:** appear to us with as little warning as a cloud in summer.

138-39. **You make me strange/ Even to the disposition that I owe:** you make me a stranger to my own nature.

Thou hast no speculation in those eyes
Which thou dost glare with!

Lady. Think of this, good peers,
But as a thing of custom. 'Tis no other.
Only it spoils the pleasure of the time.

Macb. What man dare, I dare.
Approach thou like the rugged Russian bear,
The armed rhinoceros, or the Hyrcan tiger;
Take any shape but that, and my firm nerves
Shall never tremble. Or be alive again
And dare me to the desert with thy sword.
If trembling I inhabit then, protest me
The baby of a girl. Hence, horrible shadow!
Unreal mock'ry, hence!

[*Exit Ghost.*]

Why, so! Being gone,
I am a man again. Pray you sit still.

Lady. You have displaced the mirth, broke the good meeting
With most admired disorder.

Macb. Can such things be,
And overcome us like a summer's cloud
Without our special wonder? You make me strange
Even to the disposition that I owe,
When now I think you can behold such sights
And keep the natural ruby of your cheeks
When mine is blanched with fear.

Ross. What sights, my lord?

Lady. I pray you speak not. He grows worse and worse;

147. **Stand not upon the order of your going:** that is, dispense with formality in going.

155. **Augures:** auguries, probably pronounced "augers"; predictions; **understood relations:** prophetic interpretations.

156. **maggot-pies:** magpies; **choughs:** members of the crow family. The patterns made by birds in flight were interpreted as omens.

159. **How say'st thou that:** what do you say to the fact that.

162. **I hear it by the way:** that is, his spies have so reported.

165. **betimes:** early.

171. **will to hand:** shall be carried out.

173. **season:** preservative.

174. **self-abuse:** delusion; see II. i. 59.

Question enrages him. At once, good night.
Stand not upon the order of your going,
But go at once.

Len. Good night, and better health
Attend his Majesty!

Lady. A kind good night to all!

Exeunt Lords [and Attendants].

Macb. It will have blood, they say: blood will have blood.
Stones have been known to move and trees to speak;
Augures and understood relations have
By maggot-pies and choughs and rooks brought forth
The secret'st man of blood. What is the night?

Lady. Almost at odds with morning, which is which.

Macb. How say'st thou that Macduff denies his person
At our great bidding?

Lady. Did you send to him, sir?

Macb. I hear it by the way; but I will send.
There's not a one of them but in his house
I keep a servant feed. I will tomorrow
(And betimes I will) to the Weird Sisters.
More shall they speak; for now I am bent to know
By the worst means the worst. For mine own good
All causes shall give way. I am in blood
Stepped in so far that, should I wade no more,
Returning were as tedious as go o'er.
Strange things I have in head, that will to hand,
Which must be acted ere they may be scanned.

Lady. You lack the season of all natures, sleep.

Macb. Come, we'll to sleep. My strange and self-abuse

175. **the initiate fear that wants hard use:** the timidity of a beginner who lacks the experience to be hardened in crime.

III. v. Practically no modern editor believes this scene to be authentic. The song is one contained in Thomas Middleton's *The Witch* and for this reason many have thought he was responsible for interpolations here and in other witch scenes. In any case, the scene adds nothing to the action of the play and detracts from the atmosphere which the playwright has elsewhere created.

---

2. **beldams:** hags.

7. **close:** secret.

15. **the pit of Acheron:** a river in Hell in classic mythology.

Is the initiate fear that wants hard use.
We are yet but young in deed.

Exeunt.

Scene V. [A heath.]

Thunder. Enter the three *Witches,* meeting *Hecate.*

1. Witch. Why, how now, Hecate? You look angerly.

Hec. Have I not reason, beldams as you are,
Saucy and overbold? How did you dare
To trade and traffic with Macbeth
In riddles and affairs of death;
And I, the mistress of your charms,
The close contriver of all harms,
Was never called to bear my part
Or show the glory of our art?
And, which is worse, all you have done
Hath been but for a wayward son,
Spiteful and wrathful, who, as others do,
Loves for his own ends, not for you.
But make amends now. Get you gone
And at the pit of Acheron
Meet me i' the morning. Thither he
Will come to know his destiny.
Your vessels and your spells provide,
Your charms and everything beside.
I am for the air. This night I'll spend

21. **dismal:** disastrous; see I. ii. 61.

24. **a vap'rous drop profound:** a heavy drop of moisture, ready to fall.

29. **confusion:** destruction; see II. iii. 70.

31. **grace:** virtue.

III. vi. Lennox and another Scottish lord discuss the latest happenings. Lennox ironically comments that by the logic applied to Duncan's murder, Fleance must be Banquo's murderer because he too fled the scene. It is clear that no one doubts Macbeth's guilt. The lord reports that Macduff has gone to England, where Malcolm is staying with King Edward, in the hope of raising an army to unseat Macbeth and place Malcolm on the throne. Macbeth, rebuffed when he summoned Macduff, has already made preparations for war.

---

4. **Marry:** a mild oath, originally "By the Virgin Mary." Lennox implies that Macbeth found it easy to pity Duncan once he was out of the way.

Unto a dismal and a fatal end.
Great business must be wrought ere noon.
Upon the corner of the moon
There hangs a vap'rous drop profound.
I'll catch it ere it come to ground;
And that, distilled by magic sleights,
Shall raise such artificial sprites
As by the strength of their illusion
Shall draw him on to his confusion.
He shall spurn fate, scorn death, and bear
His hopes 'bove wisdom, grace, and fear;
And you all know security
Is mortals' chiefest enemy.
Music and a song within. "Come away, come away," &c.
Hark! I am called. My little spirit, see,
Sits in a foggy cloud and stays for me. [*Exit.*]

1. Witch. Come, let's make haste. She'll soon be back again.

Exeunt.

Scene VI. [Forres. The Palace.]

Enter *Lennox* and another *Lord.*

Len. My former speeches have but hit your thoughts,
Which can interpret farther. Only I say
Things have been strangely borne. The gracious Duncan
Was pitied of Macbeth. Marry, he was dead!
And the right valiant Banquo walked too late;
Whom, you may say (if't please you) Fleance killed,

8. **Who cannot want the thought:** that is, who can fail to think.

10. **fact:** evil deed.

11. **straight:** instantly; see III. i. 156.

19. **an't:** if it.

21. **broad words:** i.e., talking too freely and boldly.

26. **holds the due of birth:** withholds the birthright.

31. **upon his aid:** in behalf of Malcolm.

32. **Siward:** Earl of Northumberland.

36. **Free from our feasts and banquets bloody knives:** that is, restore order in the state so that banquets will no longer be occasions for murder.

37. **free:** honest and disinterested.

For Fleance fled. Men must not walk too late.
Who cannot want the thought how monstrous
It was for Malcolm and for Donalbain
To kill their gracious father? Damned fact!
How it did grieve Macbeth! Did he not straight,
In pious rage, the two delinquents tear,
That were the slaves of drink and thralls of sleep?
Was not that nobly done? Ay, and wisely too!
For 'twould have angered any heart alive
To hear the men deny't. So that I say
He has borne all things well; and I do think
That, had he Duncan's sons under his key
(As, an't please heaven, he shall not), they should find
What 'twere to kill a father. So should Fleance.
But peace! for from broad words, and 'cause he failed
His presence at the tyrant's feast, I hear
Macduff lives in disgrace. Sir, can you tell
Where he bestows himself?

Lord. The son of Duncan,
From whom this tyrant holds the due of birth,
Lives in the English court, and is received
Of the most pious Edward with such grace
That the malevolence of fortune nothing
Takes from his high respect. Thither Macduff
Is gone to pray the holy King upon his aid
To wake Northumberland and warlike Siward;
That by the help of these (with Him above
To ratify the work) we may again
Give to our tables meat, sleep to our nights,
Free from our feasts and banquets bloody knives,
Do faithful homage and receive free honors—

39. **exasperate:** exasperated.

43. **cloudy:** unhappy (at having to take such an answer to Macbeth); **turns me:** i.e., turns. **Me** indicates only the speaker's interest in the circumstances described, a grammatical construction known as the "ethical dative."

45. **clogs:** hinders. The messenger won't hurry back with a negative answer.

All which we pine for now. And this report
Hath so exasperate the King that he
Prepares for some attempt of war.

Len. Sent he to Macduff?

Lord. He did; and with an absolute "Sir, not I!"
The cloudy messenger turns me his back
And hums, as who should say, "You'll rue the time
That clogs me with this answer."

Len. And that well might
Advise him to a caution t' hold what distance
His wisdom can provide. Some holy angel
Fly to the court of England and unfold
His message ere he come, that a swift blessing
May soon return to this our suffering country
Under a hand accursed!

Lord. I'll send my prayers with him.

Exeunt.

THE TRAGEDY OF

MACBETH

ACT IV

IV. i. Macbeth calls on the three witches to learn the truth about the future. They raise three apparitions, an Armed Head, a Bloody Child, and a Child Crowned bearing a tree in its hand, who tell Macbeth to beware Macduff but assure him that no man of woman born can harm him and that he cannot be defeated until Birnam Wood comes to Dunsinane. His pleasure in these prophecies is diminished, however, by the apparitions of a line of kings all resembling Banquo. When Macbeth learns that Macduff has fled to England, he determines to slaughter his family without further delay.

---

1. **brinded:** brindled, streaked.

3. **Harpier:** the Third Witch's familiar; see I. i. 9.

8. **Swelt'red:** sweated; **sleeping got:** created while sleeping.

12. **fenny snake:** snake which inhabits fens.

16. **blindworm:** a small lizard; actually harmless.

17. **howlet:** owlet.

ACT IV

Scene I. [A cavern. In the middle, a boiling cauldron.]

Thunder. Enter the three *Witches.*

1. Witch. Thrice the brinded cat hath mewed.
2. Witch. Thrice, and once the hedge-pig whined.
3. Witch. Harpier cries; 'tis time, 'tis time.
1. Witch. Round about the cauldron go;
In the poisoned entrails throw.
Toad, that under cold stone
Days and nights has thirty-one
Swelt'red venom sleeping got,
Boil thou first i' the charmed pot.
All. Double, double, toil and trouble;
Fire burn, and cauldron bubble.
2. Witch. Fillet of a fenny snake,
In the cauldron boil and bake;
Eye of newt, and toe of frog,
Wool of bat, and tongue of dog,
Adder's fork, and blindworm's sting,
Lizard's leg, and howlet's wing;
For a charm of pow'rful trouble
Like a hell-broth boil and bubble.
All. Double, double, toil and trouble;
Fire burn, and cauldron bubble.

23. **Witch's mummy:** a fragment of the mummified body of a witch. **Mummy** was a general term for the specially treated flesh of corpses to which was attributed magical powers; **maw and gulf:** stomach and gullet; see III. iv. 89.

24. **ravined:** voracious.

25. **digged i' the dark:** i.e., dug up when it would have the greatest potency. Midnight was supposed to be the most favorable time for collecting herbs for magic purposes.

31. **drab:** whore.

32. **slab:** sticky, slimy.

33. **chaudron:** entrails.

S.D. after l. 38. **Hecate and the other three Witches:** Hecate's appearance here is generally believed to be another interpolation. The **other three Witches** were probably needed for the stage business accompanying the song. No specific exit is provided for them, but they may be included in the Stage Direction after l. 147.

3. Witch. Scale of dragon, tooth of wolf,
Witch's mummy, maw and gulf
Of the ravined salt-sea shark,
Root of hemlock, digged i' the dark;
Liver of blaspheming Jew,
Gall of goat, and slips of yew
Slivered in the moon's eclipse;
Nose of Turk and Tartar's lips;
Finger of birth-strangled babe
Ditch-delivered by a drab:
Make the gruel thick and slab.
Add thereto a tiger's chaudron
For the ingredience of our cauldron.
All. Double, double, toil and trouble;
Fire burn, and cauldron bubble.
2. Witch. Cool it with a baboon's blood,
Then the charm is firm and good.

Enter *Hecate* and the other three *Witches.*

Hec. O, well done! I commend your pains,
And every one shall share i' the gains.
And now about the cauldron sing
Like elves and fairies in a ring,
Enchanting all that you put in.
Music and a song, "Black spirit," &c.
2. Witch. By the pricking of my thumbs,
Something wicked this way comes.
Open locks,
Whoever knocks!

52. **by that which you profess:** i.e., by your magic art.

55. **yesty:** yeasty, foaming.

56. **Confound:** destroy; see II. ii. 15.

57. **bladed corn:** ripe wheat; **lodged:** beaten flat.

61. **nature's germens:** the seeds of everything yet uncreated.

A witch raising demons.

From Olaus Magnus, *Historia de gentibus septentrionalibus* (1555).

Enter *Macbeth.*

Macb. How now, you secret, black, and midnight hags?
What is't you do?
All. A deed without a name.
Macb. I conjure you by that which you profess
(Howe'er you come to know it), answer me.
Though you untie the winds and let them fight
Against the churches; though the yesty waves
Confound and swallow navigation up;
Though bladed corn be lodged and trees blown down;
Though castles topple on their warders' heads;
Though palaces and pyramids do slope
Their heads to their foundations; though the treasure
Of nature's germens tumble all together,
Even till destruction sicken—answer me
To what I ask you.
1. Witch. Speak.
2. Witch. Demand.
3. Witch. We'll answer.
1. Witch. Say, if th' hadst rather hear it from our mouths
Or from our masters.
Macb. Call 'em! Let me see 'em.
1. Witch. Pour in sow's blood, that hath eaten
Her nine farrow; grease that's sweaten
From the murderer's gibbet throw
Into the flame.
All. Come, high or low;
Thyself and office deftly show!

S.D. after l. 76. **an Armed Head:** symbolic of Macbeth's coming combat with Macduff.

84. **harped:** struck the right note, guessed.

S.D. after l. 86. **a Bloody Child:** symbolizing Macduff, untimely ripped from his mother's womb. Macbeth does not yet realize the significance of this symbol.

94. **take a bond of fate:** bind fate by a contract.

Thunder. First Apparition, an Armed Head.

Macb. Tell me, thou unknown power—
1. Witch. He knows thy thought.
Hear his speech, but say thou naught.
1. Appar. Macbeth! Macbeth! Macbeth! Beware Macduff;
Beware the Thane of Fife. Dismiss me. Enough.
He descends.
Macb. Whate'er thou art, for thy good caution thanks!
Thou hast harped my fear aright. But one word more—
1. Witch. He will not be commanded. Here's another,
More potent than the first.

Thunder. Second Apparition, a Bloody Child.

2. Appar. Macbeth! Macbeth! Macbeth!
Macb. Had I three ears, I'ld hear thee.
2. Appar. Be bloody, bold, and resolute; laugh to scorn
The pow'r of man, for none of woman born
Shall harm Macbeth.
Descends.
Macb. Then live, Macduff. What need I fear of thee?
But yet I'll make assurance double sure
And take a bond of fate. Thou shalt not live!
That I may tell pale-hearted fear it lies
And sleep in spite of thunder.

S.D. after l. 96. **a Child Crowned:** Duncan's son Malcolm, bearing a symbol of his subterfuge to surprise Macbeth by disguising his men as trees. Again Macbeth is unaware of the apparition's significance.

108. **impress:** draft.

109. **bodements:** omens.

113. **mortal custom:** the normal mortality of human beings.

120. **noise:** a common word for "music."

Thunder. Third Apparition, a Child Crowned, with a tree in his hand.

What is this
That rises like the issue of a king
And wears upon his baby-brow the round
And top of sovereignty?
All. Listen, but speak not to't.
3. *Appar.* Be lion-mettled, proud, and take no care
Who chafes, who frets, or where conspirers are.
Macbeth shall never vanquished be until
Great Birnam Wood to high Dunsinane Hill
Shall come against him. *Descends.*
Macb. That will never be.
Who can impress the forest, bid the tree
Unfix his earth-bound root? Sweet bodements, good!
Rebellious dead rise never till the Wood
Of Birnam rise, and our high-placed Macbeth
Shall live the lease of nature, pay his breath
To time and mortal custom. Yet my heart
Throbs to know one thing. Tell me, if your art
Can tell so much—shall Banquo's issue ever
Reign in this kingdom?
All. Seek to know no more.
Macb. I will be satisfied. Deny me this,
And an eternal curse fall on you! Let me know.
Why sinks that cauldron? and what noise is this?
Hautboys.
1. *Witch.* Show!
2. *Witch.* Show!
3. *Witch.* Show!

S.D. after l. 125. **glass:** mirror.

135. **twofold balls and treble scepters:** the orb and scepter are the emblems of sovereignty. The two orbs and three scepters signify rule over Scotland as well as England beginning with James I. Two scepters were conventionally used in English coronation rites.

137. **blood-boltered:** with blood matting his hair.

142. **sprites:** spirits; see II. iii. 85.

145. **antic round:** grotesque dance in a circle.

A witch raising a storm.

From Olaus Magnus, *Historia de gentibus septentrionalibus* (1555).

All. Show his eyes, and grieve his heart!
Come like shadows, so depart!

A show of eight Kings, [the eighth] with a glass in his hand, and Banquo last.

Macb. Thou art too like the spirit of Banquo. Down!
Thy crown does sear mine eyeballs. And thy hair,
Thou other gold-bound brow, is like the first.
A third is like the former. Filthy hags!
Why do you show me this? A fourth? Start, eyes!
What, will the line stretch out to the crack of doom?
Another yet? A seventh? I'll see no more.
And yet the eighth appears, who bears a glass
Which shows me many more; and some I see
That twofold balls and treble scepters carry.
Horrible sight! Now I see 'tis true;
For the blood-boltered Banquo smiles upon me
And points at them for his. [*Apparitions descend.*] What?
Is this so?
1. Witch. Ay, sir, all this is so. But why
Stands Macbeth thus amazedly?
Come, sisters, cheer we up his sprites
And show the best of our delights.
I'll charm the air to give a sound
While you perform your antic round,
That this great king may kindly say
Our duties did his welcome pay.
Music. The Witches dance, and vanish.
Macb. Where are they? Gone? Let this pernicious hour
Stand aye accursed in the calendar!
Come in, without there!

165-66. **The flighty purpose never is o'ertook/ Unless the deed go with it:** so swift is purpose that it will escape completely unless it is carried out at once.

173. **trace:** follow; i.e., succeed.

Enter *Lennox.*

Len. What's your Grace's will?
Macb. Saw you the Weird Sisters?
Len. No, my lord.
Macb. Came they not by you?
Len. No indeed, my lord.
Macb. Infected be the air whereon they ride,
And damned all those that trust them! I did hear
The galloping of horse. Who was't came by?
Len. 'Tis two or three, my lord, that bring you word
Macduff is fled to England.
Macb. Fled to England?
Len. Ay, my good lord.
Macb. [*Aside*] Time, thou anticipat'st my dread exploits.
The flighty purpose never is o'ertook
Unless the deed go with it. From this moment
The very firstlings of my heart shall be
The firstlings of my hand. And even now,
To crown my thoughts with acts, be it thought and done!
The castle of Macduff I will surprise,
Seize upon Fife, give to the edge o' the sword
His wife, his babes, and all unfortunate souls
That trace him in his line. No boasting like a fool!
This deed I'll do before this purpose cool.
But no more sights!—Where are these gentlemen?
Come, bring me where they are.

Exeunt.

IV. ii. Ross tries to comfort Lady Macduff, who cannot understand her husband's desertion. She is warned by a messenger to fly but he has no sooner left than Macbeth's hired assassins arrive and carry out his instructions to kill Macduff's family.

4-5. **When our actions do not,/ Our fears do make us traitors:** though we may not act traitorously, displaying fear betrays the treason in our hearts.

11. **wants the natural touch:** lacks the natural instinct to protect his wife and children.

17. **coz:** cousin, kinswoman.

18. **school:** control.

20. **fits o' the season:** disorders of the present era.

21-2. **we are traitors/ And do not know ourselves:** we are treated as traitors and are conscious of no treason.

22-3. **hold rumor/ From what we fear:** believe what our fears dictate.

26. **Shall not:** that is, the time shall not.

this scene to show humorous mother & son—so we will feel compassion when they murder

Scene II. [Fife. Macduff's Castle.]

Enter *Macduff's Wife*, her *Son*, and *Ross*.

Wife. What had he done to make him fly the land?
Ross. You must have patience, madam.
Wife. He had none.
His flight was madness. When our actions do not,
Our fears do make us traitors.
Ross. You know not
Whether it was his wisdom or his fear.
Wife. Wisdom? To leave his wife, to leave his babes,
His mansion, and his titles, in a place
From whence himself does fly? He loves us not,
He wants the natural touch. For the poor wren,
(The most diminutive of birds) will fight,
Her young ones in her nest, against the owl.
All is the fear, and nothing is the love,
As little is the wisdom, where the flight
So runs against all reason.
Ross. My dearest coz,
I pray you school yourself. But for your husband,
He is noble, wise, judicious, and best knows
The fits o' the season. I dare not speak much further;
But cruel are the times, when we are traitors
And do not know ourselves; when we hold rumor
From what we fear, yet know not what we fear,
But float upon a wild and violent sea
Each way and move—I take my leave of you.
Shall not be long but I'll be here again.

27. **cease:** stand still.

32. **my disgrace and your discomfort:** i.e., he would be moved to tears by their plight.

39. **lime:** birdlime, a sticky substance used to catch birds.

40. **gin:** snare.

41-2. **Poor birds they are not set for:** that is, traps are not set for birds of little worth.

47. **sell:** betray.

49. **wit enough for thee:** enough intelligence for a child so young.

humorous scene

Things at the worst will cease, or else climb upward
To what they were before.—My pretty cousin,
Blessing upon you!
Wife. Fathered he is, and yet he's fatherless.
Ross. I am so much a fool, should I stay longer,
It would be my disgrace and your discomfort.
I take my leave at once. *Exit.*
Wife. Sirrah, your father's dead;
And what will you do now? How will you live?
Son. As birds do, mother.
Wife. What, with worms and flies?
Son. With what I get, I mean; and so do they.
Wife. Poor bird! thou'dst never fear the net nor lime,
The pitfall nor the gin.
Son. Why should I, mother? Poor birds they are not set for.
My father is not dead, for all your saying.
Wife. Yes, he is dead. How wilt thou do for a father?
Son. Nay, how will you do for a husband?
Wife. Why, I can buy me twenty at any market.
Son. Then you'll buy 'em to sell again.
Wife. Thou speak'st with all thy wit; and yet, i' faith,
With wit enough for thee.
Son. Was my father a traitor, mother?
Wife. Ay, that he was!
Son. What is a traitor?
Wife. Why, one that swears, and lies.
Son. And be all traitors that do so?
Wife. Every one that does so is a traitor and must be hanged.
Son. And must they all be hanged that swear and lie?

62. **enow:** enough.

71. **in your state of honor I am perfect:** I know you well for a noble lady.

72. **doubt:** fear.

76. **fell:** deadly; see I. v. 50.

82. **sometime:** sometimes.

Wife. Every one.

Son. Who must hang them?

Wife. Why, the honest men.

Son. Then the liars and swearers are fools; for there are liars and swearers enow to beat the honest men and hang up them.

Wife. Now God help thee, poor monkey!
But how wilt thou do for a father?

Son. If he were dead, you'ld weep for him. If you would not, it were a good sign that I should quickly have a new father.

Wife. Poor prattler, how thou talk'st!

Enter a *Messenger*.

Mess. Bless you, fair dame! I am not to you known,
Though in your state of honor I am perfect.
I doubt some danger does approach you nearly.
If you will take a homely man's advice,
Be not found here. Hence with your little ones!
To fright you thus methinks I am too savage;
To do worse to you were fell cruelty,
Which is too nigh your person. Heaven preserve you!
I dare abide no longer. *Exit*.

Wife. Whither should I fly?
I have done no harm. But I remember now
I am in this earthly world, where to do harm
Is often laudable, to do good sometime
Accounted dangerous folly. Why then, alas,
Do I put up that womanly defense
To say I have done no harm?—What are these faces?

90. **shag-eared:** with long, shaggy hair falling about his ears.

IV. iii. Macduff has sought out Malcolm to urge him to depose Macbeth and take over Scotland's rule. Malcolm is distrustful, fearing that Macduff is a tool of Macbeth, but is finally convinced by his sincerity and tells him that the Earl of Northumberland with an army of ten thousand is ready to set out. Ross appears and reports that revolts have already begun against Macbeth's tyrannical rule. Macduff, hearing of his family's fate, resolves to avenge their murder upon Macbeth.

5. **Bestride our downfall'n birthdom:** fight to protect our country, which has been beaten to its knees.

9. **Like syllable of dolor:** similar anguished cries.

Enter *Murderers.*

Mur. Where is your husband?
Wife. I hope, in no place so unsanctified
Where such as thou mayst find him.
Mur. He's a traitor.
Son. Thou liest, thou shag-eared villain!
Mur. What, you egg! [*Stabbing him.*]
Young fry of treachery!
Son. He has killed me, mother.
Run away, I pray you! [*Dies.*]
Exit [*Lady Macduff*], *crying* "Murder!" [*followed by Murderers.*]

Scene III. [England. Before the King's Palace.]

Enter *Malcolm* and *Macduff.*

Mal. Let us seek out some desolate shade, and there
Weep our sad bosoms empty.
Macd. Let us rather
Hold fast the mortal sword and, like good men,
Bestride our downfall'n birthdom. Each new morn
New widows howl, new orphans cry, new sorrows
Strike heaven on the face, that it resounds
As if it felt with Scotland and yelled out
Like syllable of dolor.
Mal. What I believe, I'll wail;

12. **the time to friend:** favorable opportunity.

14. **sole name:** name alone.

15. **honest:** honorable, of good character.

17. **You may discern of him through me:** i.e., by betraying me to him; **and wisdom:** and think it wisdom.

22-3. **recoil/ In an imperial charge:** turn to avoid the displeasure of a sovereign.

23-4. **I shall crave your pardon./ That which you are, my thoughts cannot transpose:** you must excuse me. In any case, my suspicions cannot change what you are; so I have not harmed you.

25. **the brightest:** Lucifer.

26-7. **Though all things foul would wear the brows of grace,/ Yet grace must still look so:** though everything foul should simulate the appearance of virtue, yet there is no other way for virtue to look except like itself.

30. **in that rawness:** so hastily, without proper care for their protection.

31. **motives:** inspirations.

33-4. **Let not my jealousies be your dishonors,/ But mine own safeties:** that is, my suspicions are not intended to insult you but to assure my own protection; **rightly just:** as honorable as you appear.

37. **basis:** foundation.

38-9. **Wear thou thy wrongs;/ The title is affeered:** keep your stolen honors, your right to

[continued

Vhat know, believe; and what I can redress,
ıs I shall find the time to friend, I will.
Vhat you have spoke, it may be so perchance.
'his tyrant, whose sole name blisters our tongues,
Vas once thought honest; you have loved him well;
Ie hath not touched you yet. I am young; but something
ou may discern of him through me, and wisdom
'o offer up a weak, poor, innocent lamb
" appease an angry god.
Macd. I am not treacherous.
Mal. But Macbeth is.
ı good and virtuous nature may recoil
n an imperial charge. But I shall crave your pardon.
'hat which you are, my thoughts cannot transpose.
ıngels are bright still, though the brightest fell.
Though all things foul would wear the brows of grace,
'et grace must still look so.
Macd. I have lost my hopes.
Mal. Perchance even there where I did find my doubts.
Why in that rawness left you wife and child,
Those precious motives, those strong knots of love,
Without leave-taking? I pray you,
.et not my jealousies be your dishonors,
3ut mine own safeties. You may be rightly just,
Whatever I shall think.
Macd. Bleed, bleed, poor country!
Great tyranny, lay thou thy basis sure,
For goodness dare not check thee! Wear thou thy wrongs;
The title is affeered! Fare thee well, lord.
I would not be the villain that thou think'st

them is legally certified **(affeered). Affeered** is a legal term meaning certified, but a pun on affeered/ afeard (afraid) may be intended.

49. **gracious England:** i.e., the English King, Edward the Confessor.

58. **particulars:** particular kinds; **grafted:** that is, like species of plants.

59. **opened:** budded open.

62. **confineless:** unlimited.

67. **Luxurious:** lustful.

68. **Sudden:** violent.

For the whole space that's in the tyrant's grasp
And the rich East to boot.
Mal. Be not offended.
I speak not as in absolute fear of you.
I think our country sinks beneath the yoke;
It weeps, it bleeds, and each new day a gash
Is added to her wounds. I think withal
There would be hands uplifted in my right;
And here from gracious England have I offer
Of goodly thousands. But, for all this,
When I shall tread upon the tyrant's head
Or wear it on my sword, yet my poor country
Shall have more vices than it had before,
More suffer and more sundry ways than ever,
By him that shall succeed.
Macd. What should he be?
Mal. It is myself I mean; in whom I know
All the particulars of vice so grafted
That, when they shall be opened, black Macbeth
Will seem as pure as snow, and the poor state
Esteem him as a lamb, being compared
With my confineless harms.
Macd. Not in the legions
Of horrid hell can come a devil more damned
In evils to top Macbeth.
Mal. I grant him bloody,
Luxurious, avaricious, false, deceitful,
Sudden, malicious, smacking of every sin
That has a name. But there's no bottom, none,
In my voluptuousness. Your wives, your daughters,
Your matrons, and your maids could not fill up

73. **continent:** (1) chaste; (2) restraining.

76-7. **Boundless intemperance/ In nature is a tyranny:** boundless intemperance usurps man's natural rule of himself.

81. **Convey:** manage in secret fashion. The word was often used in the sense of "steal."

82. **the time:** i.e., everyone; see I. v. 71.

88. **affection:** disposition.

93. **forge:** fabricate.

98. **summer-seeming:** as quick of growth as summer flowers and as brief.

100. **foisons:** plenty.

101. **your mere own:** what unquestionably belongs to you; **portable:** bearable.

102. **With other graces weighed:** balancing (against these vices) your other virtues.

The cistern of my lust; and my desire
All continent impediments would o'erbear
That did oppose my will. Better Macbeth
Than such an one to reign.

Macd. Boundless intemperance
In nature is a tyranny. It hath been
The untimely emptying of the happy throne
And fall of many kings. But fear not yet
To take upon you what is yours. You may
Convey your pleasures in a spacious plenty,
And yet seem cold—the time you may so hoodwink.
We have willing dames enough. There cannot be
That vulture in you to devour so many
As will to greatness dedicate themselves,
Finding it so inclined.

Mal. With this there grows
In my most ill-composed affection such
A stanchless avarice that, were I King,
I should cut off the nobles for their lands,
Desire his jewels, and this other's house,
And my more-having would be as a sauce
To make me hunger more, that I should forge
Quarrels unjust against the good and loyal,
Destroying them for wealth.

Macd. This avarice
Sticks deeper, grows with more pernicious root
Than summer-seeming lust; and it hath been
The sword of our slain kings. Yet do not fear.
Scotland hath foisons to fill up your will
Of your mere own. All these are portable,
With other graces weighed.

107. **relish:** taste, suggestion.

108. **several:** separate.

111. **Uproar:** change to uproar.

120: **Since that:** since.

121. **interdiction:** ban. Shakespeare may also have known of the sense of the word in Scottish law: "a restraint [sometimes voluntary] imposed upon a person incapable of managing his own affairs."

122. **blaspheme his breed:** slander his begetters.

125. **Died:** i.e., denied earthly life.

130. **Child of:** i.e., proceeding directly from.

131. **scruples:** doubts; see II. iii. 149.

133. **these trains:** tricks such as I have suspected you of.

Mal. But I have none. The king-becoming graces,
As justice, verity, temp'rance, stableness,
Bounty, perseverance, mercy, lowliness,
Devotion, patience, courage, fortitude,
I have no relish of them, but abound
In the division of each several crime,
Acting it many ways. Nay, had I pow'r, I should
Pour the sweet milk of concord into hell,
Uproar the universal peace, confound
All unity on earth.
Macd. O Scotland, Scotland!
Mal. If such a one be fit to govern, speak.
I am as I have spoken.
Macd. Fit to govern?
No, not to live. O nation miserable,
With an untitled tyrant bloody-scept'red,
When shalt thou see thy wholesome days again,
Since that the truest issue of thy throne
By his own interdiction stands accursed
And does blaspheme his breed? Thy royal father
Was a most sainted king; the queen that bore thee,
Oft'ner upon her knees than on her feet,
Died every day she lived. Fare thee well!
These evils thou repeat'st upon thyself
Have banished me from Scotland. O my breast,
Thy hope ends here!
Mal. Macduff, this noble passion,
Child of integrity, hath from my soul
Wiped the black scruples, reconciled my thoughts
To thy good truth and honor. Devilish Macbeth
By many of these trains hath sought to win me

134. **modest:** prudent.

150. **at a point:** armed and ready for action.

151-52. **the chance of goodness/ Be like our warranted quarrel:** may our chance of good luck equal the justice of our cause.

158. **stay his cure:** wait for him to cure them; **convinces:** conquers; see I. vii. 72.

159. **The great assay of art:** medicine's best efforts.

Edward the Confessor touching.

From *La estoire de Seint Aedward le Rei . . . reproduced from the unique MS.* (1920).

Into his power; and modest wisdom plucks me
From over-credulous haste; but God above
Deal between thee and me! for even now
I put myself to thy direction and
Unspeak mine own detraction, here abjure
The taints and blames I laid upon myself
For strangers to my nature. I am yet
Unknown to woman, never was forsworn,
Scarcely have coveted what was mine own,
At no time broke my faith, would not betray
The devil to his fellow, and delight
No less in truth than life. My first false speaking
Was this upon myself. What I am truly,
Is thine and my poor country's to command;
Whither indeed, before thy here-approach,
Old Siward with ten thousand warlike men
Already at a point was setting forth.
Now we'll together; and the chance of goodness
Be like our warranted quarrel! Why are you silent?
Macd. Such welcome and unwelcome things at once
'Tis hard to reconcile.

Enter a *Doctor*.

Mal. Well, more anon. Comes the King forth, I pray you?

Doct. Ay, sir. There are a crew of wretched souls
That stay his cure. Their malady convinces
The great assay of art; but at his touch,
Such sanctity hath heaven given his hand,
They presently amend.

164. **the evil:** scrofula was known as "the King's Evil," and Holinshed describes King Edward's success at "touching" to cure it, which he was believed to have bequeathed to his successors. James I was less eager to perform the rite of touching for the evil than some monarchs, but the practice continued as late as the reign of Queen Anne, by whom Samuel Johnson was touched in 1712.

168. **strangely-visited:** afflicted with extraordinary ailments.

170. **mere:** absolute; see l. 101.

171. **stamp:** coin. English monarchs from Henry VII on used the angel for this purpose, and James I at times had special mintings of such coins for the express purpose of distributing to those he touched. By his time the angel was worth ten to eleven shillings, which may in part explain King James's reluctance to perform the ceremony of healing.

172. **spoken:** i.e., generally believed.

174. **virtue:** healing ability.

182. **The means that makes us strangers:** i.e., Macbeth, the cause of our separation.

Mal. I thank you, doctor.
Exit [*Doctor*].
Macd. What's the disease he means?
Mal. 'Tis called the evil:
A most miraculous work in this good king,
Which often since my here-remain in England
I have seen him do. How he solicits heaven
Himself best knows; but strangely-visited people,
All swol'n and ulcerous, pitiful to the eye,
The mere despair of surgery, he cures,
Hanging a golden stamp about their necks,
Put on with holy prayers; and 'tis spoken,
To the succeeding royalty he leaves
The healing benediction. With this strange virtue,
He hath a heavenly gift of prophecy,
And sundry blessings hang about his throne
That speak him full of grace.

Enter *Ross.*

Macd. See who comes here.
Mal. My countryman; but yet I know him not.
Macd. My ever gentle cousin, welcome hither.
Mal. I know him now. Good God betimes remove
The means that makes us strangers!
Ross. Sir, amen.
Macd. Stands Scotland where it did?
Ross. Alas, poor country,
Almost afraid to know itself! It cannot
Be called our mother, but our grave; where nothing,
But who knows nothing, is once seen to smile;

190. **made, not marked:** that is, so common as to go unnoticed.

191. **modern:** ordinary; **ecstasy:** emotion.

192. **Is there scarce asked for who:** hardly provokes any curiosity as to who has died.

194. **or ere they sicken:** before they sicken; i.e., unnaturally by violence.

196. **nice:** scrupulously accurate, painfully detailed.

198. **doth hiss the speaker:** earns the teller nothing but hisses for repeating an old story.

199. **teems:** generates, brings to birth.

208. **heavily:** sorrowfully.

209. **out:** risen in arms.

210-11. **witnessed the rather/ For that:** confirmed all the more because.

218-19. **none/ That Christendom gives out:** there is none renowned in Christendom.

The coin called an angel.

Where sighs and groans, and shrieks that rent the air,
Are made, not marked; where violent sorrow seems
A modern ecstasy. The dead man's knell
Is there scarce asked for who; and good men's lives
Expire before the flowers in their caps,
Dying or ere they sicken.

Macd. O, relation
Too nice, and yet too true!

Mal. What's the newest grief?

Ross. That of an hour's age doth hiss the speaker;
Each minute teems a new one.

Macd. How does my wife?

Ross. Why, well.

Macd. And all my children?

Ross. Well too.

Macd. The tyrant has not battered at their peace?

Ross. No, they were well at peace when I did leave 'em.

Macd. Be not a niggard of your speech. How goes't?

Ross. When I came hither to transport the tidings
Which I have heavily borne, there ran a rumor
Of many worthy fellows that were out;
Which was to my belief witnessed the rather
For that I saw the tyrant's power afoot.
Now is the time of help. Your eye in Scotland
Would create soldiers, make our women fight
To doff their dire distresses.

Mal. Be't their comfort
We are coming thither. Gracious England hath
Lent us good Siward and ten thousand men.
An older and a better soldier none
That Christendom gives out.

223. **latch:** catch.

225. **fee-grief:** private sorrow.

226. **Due:** belonging.

233. **heaviest:** saddest; see 1. 208.

238. **quarry:** heap of dead, the spoil of the hunt.

243. **Whispers:** i.e., whispers to; **o'erfraught:** overfreighted, overcharged.

247. **must be:** had to be; that is, and it had to happen while I was away?

Ross. Would I could answer
This comfort with the like! But I have words
That would be howled out in the desert air,
Where hearing should not latch them.
Macd. What concern they?
The general cause? or is it a fee-grief
Due to some single breast?
Ross. No mind that's honest
But in it shares some woe, though the main part
Pertains to you alone.
Macd. If it be mine,
Keep it not from me, quickly let me have it.
Ross. Let not your ears despise my tongue for ever,
Which shall possess them with the heaviest sound
That ever yet they heard.
Macd. Humh! I guess at it.
Ross. Your castle is surprised; your wife and babes
Savagely slaughtered. To relate the manner
Were, on the quarry of these murdered deer,
To add the death of you.
Mal. Merciful heaven!
What, man! Ne'er pull your hat upon your brows.
Give sorrow words. The grief that does not speak
Whispers the o'erfraught heart and bids it break.
Macd. My children too?
Ross. Wife, children, servants, all
That could be found.
Macd. And I must be from thence?
My wife killed too?
Ross. I have said.
Mal. Be comforted.

257. **Dispute it like a man:** that is, do not grieve, rouse yourself to vengeance.

263. **Naught:** worthless.

270. **Front to front:** face to face.

274. **tune:** Nicholas Rowe's emendation of the Folios' "time."

276. **Our lack is nothing but our leave:** we have everything except the King's permission to go.

278. **Put on their instruments:** prepare for action.

Let's make us med'cines of our great revenge
To cure this deadly grief.
Macd. He has no children. All my pretty ones?
Did you say all? O hell-kite! All?
What, all my pretty chickens and their dam
At one fell swoop?
Mal. Dispute it like a man.
Macd. I shall do so;
But I must also feel it as a man.
I cannot but remember such things were
That were most precious to me. Did heaven look on
And would not take their part? Sinful Macduff,
They were all struck for thee! Naught that I am,
Not for their own demerits, but for mine,
Fell slaughter on their souls. Heaven rest them now!
Mal. Be this the whetstone of your sword. Let grief
Convert to anger; blunt not the heart, enrage it.
Macd. O, I could play the woman with mine eyes
And braggart with my tongue! But, gentle heavens,
Cut short all intermission. Front to front
Bring thou this fiend of Scotland and myself.
Within my sword's length set him. If he scape,
Heaven forgive him too!
Mal. This tune goes manly.
Come, go we to the King. Our power is ready;
Our lack is nothing but our leave. Macbeth
Is ripe for shaking, and the pow'rs above
Put on their instruments. Receive what cheer you may.
The night is long that never finds the day.

Exeunt.

THE TRAGEDY OF

MACBETH

ACT V

V. i. An attendant of Lady Macbeth has sought out a doctor for advice about her strange nocturnal walkings and together they observe her. She goes through the motions of washing her hands and relives the murder of Duncan. Though the observers cannot interpret all her actions, they are aware that something weighs heavily on her conscience, and the doctor leaves orders that she be carefully watched, for he fears suicide.

5. **closet:** usually a private chamber, but here probably a chest or other container for private belongings.

9. **do the effects of watching:** behave as though awake.

13. **meet:** suitable.

16. **guise:** usual manner.

17. **close:** hidden; see III. v. 7.

ACT V

Scene I. [Dunsinane. Macbeth's Castle.]

Enter a *Doctor of Physic* and a *Waiting Gentlewoman.*

Doct. I have two nights watched with you, but can perceive no truth in your report. When was it she last walked?

Gent. Since his Majesty went into the field I have seen her rise from her bed, throw her nightgown upon her, unlock her closet, take forth paper, fold it, write upon't, read it, afterwards seal it, and again return to bed; yet all this while in a most fast sleep.

Doct. A great perturbation in nature, to receive at once the benefit of sleep and do the effects of watching! In this slumb'ry agitation, besides her walking and other actual performances, what (at any time) have you heard her say?

Gent. That, sir, which I will not report after her.

Doct. You may to me, and 'tis most meet you should.

Gent. Neither to you nor any one, having no witness to confirm my speech.

Enter *Lady* [*Macbeth*], with a taper.

Lo you, here she comes! This is her very guise, and, upon my life, fast asleep! Observe her; stand close.

Doct. How came she by that light?

34. **accompt:** account.
42. **Go to:** for shame.

Gent. Why, it stood by her. She has light by her continually. 'Tis her command.

Doct. You see her eyes are open.

Gent. Ay, but their sense is shut.

Doct. What is it she does now? Look how she rubs her hands.

Gent. It is an accustomed action with her, to seem thus washing her hands. I have known her continue in this a quarter of an hour.

Lady. Yet here's a spot.

Doct. Hark, she speaks! I will set down what comes from her, to satisfy my remembrance the more strongly.

Lady. Out, damned spot! out, I say! One; two. Why then 'tis time to do't. Hell is murky. Fie, my lord, fie! a soldier, and afeard? What need we fear who knows it, when none can call our pow'r to accompt? Yet who would have thought the old man to have had so much blood in him?

Doct. Do you mark that?

Lady. The Thane of Fife had a wife. Where is she now? What, will these hands ne'er be clean? No more o' that, my lord, no more o' that! You mar all with this starting.

Doct. Go to, go to! You have known what you should not.

Gent. She has spoke what she should not, I am sure of that. Heaven knows what she has known.

Lady. Here's the smell of the blood still. All the perfumes of Arabia will not sweeten this little hand. Oh, oh, oh!

59. **on's:** of his.

71. **annoyance:** injury.

73. **mated:** overcome, bewildered; **amazed:** overcome with confusion; see II. iii. 122.

Doct. What a sigh is there! The heart is sorely charged.

Gent. I would not have such a heart in my bosom for the dignity of the whole body.

Doct. Well, well, well.

Gent. Pray God it be, sir.

Doct. This disease is beyond my practice. Yet I have known those which have walked in their sleep who have died holily in their beds.

Lady. Wash your hands, put on your nightgown, look not so pale! I tell you yet again, Banquo's buried. He cannot come out on's grave.

Doct. Even so?

Lady. To bed, to bed! There's knocking at the gate. Come, come, come, come, give me your hand! What's done cannot be undone. To bed, to bed, to bed! *Exit.*

Doct. Will she go now to bed?

Gent. Directly.

Doct. Foul whisp'rings are abroad. Unnatural deeds
Do breed unnatural troubles. Infected minds
To their deaf pillows will discharge their secrets.
More needs she the divine than the physician.
God, God forgive us all! Look after her;
Remove from her the means of all annoyance,
And still keep eyes upon her. So good night.
My mind she has mated, and amazed my sight.
I think, but dare not speak.

Gent. Good night, good doctor.

Exeunt.

V. ii. A body of Scottish rebels against Macbeth approach Birnam Wood, where they are to meet Malcolm and his English forces. They have heard that Macbeth has fortified Dunsinane and is prepared to defend it with fury, but that he lacks the loyalty of his own men.

---

3. **dear:** deeply felt.

4. **bleeding and the grim alarm:** bloody and desperate attack.

5. **mortified:** usually used in the sense of "deadened" or "paralyzed," but probably it means literally dead here.

7. **well:** likely.

11. **unrough:** smooth-faced, beardless.

17-8. **He cannot buckle his distempered cause/ Within the belt of rule:** Macbeth is pictured as a man so swollen with disease that he cannot fasten his belt; i.e., his cause is so wicked that he cannot support it with the calm of a man who knows himself to be in the right.

21. **minutely:** every minute; **faith-breach:** his breach of faith in killing the King.

Scene II. [The country near Dunsinane.]

Drum and Colors. Enter *Menteith, Caithness, Angus, Lennox, Soldiers.*

Ment. The English pow'r is near, led on by Malcolm,
His uncle Siward, and the good Macduff.
Revenges burn in them; for their dear causes
Would to the bleeding and the grim alarm
Excite the mortified man.
Ang. Near Birnam Wood
Shall we well meet them; that way are they coming.
Caith. Who knows if Donalbain be with his brother?
Len. For certain, sir, he is not. I have a file
Of all the gentry. There is Siward's son
And many unrough youths that even now
Protest their first of manhood.
Ment. What does the tyrant?
Caith. Great Dunsinane he strongly fortifies.
Some say he's mad; others, that lesser hate him,
Do call it valiant fury; but for certain
He cannot buckle his distempered cause
Within the belt of rule.
Ang. Now does he feel
His secret murders sticking on his hands.
Now minutely revolts upbraid his faith-breach.
Those he commands move only in command,
Nothing in love. Now does he feel his title
Hang loose about him, like a giant's robe
Upon a dwarfish thief.

27. **pestered:** harassed.

28-9. **When all that is within him does condemn/ Itself for being there:** when his mind is stored only with guilty recollections.

32. **med'cine:** i.e., Malcolm; **weal:** commonwealth, state; see III. iv. 94.

33. **purge:** cleansing, by bloodletting; i.e., let us purge our country of its sickness if we have to drain every drop of our blood.

36. **dew:** water; **sovereign flower:** Malcolm, the rightful King.

V. iii. Macbeth awaits the attack, confident that he has been promised safety. Since he has none of the usual pleasures of old age to look forward to, he does not fear death. Lady Macbeth is now in the doctor's constant care, but he can do little to cure her troubled mind.

---

3. **taint:** become tainted.

5. **All mortal consequences:** all human events.

8. **English epicures:** the English were believed to be fond of rich diet while the Scots ate plainer food.

9. **sway by:** rule myself with.

Ment. Who then shall blame
His pestered senses to recoil and start,
When all that is within him does condemn
Itself for being there?
Caith. Well, march we on
To give obedience where 'tis truly owed.
Meet we the med'cine of the sickly weal;
And with him pour we in our country's purge
Each drop of us.
Len. Or so much as it needs
To dew the sovereign flower and drown the weeds.
Make we our march towards Birnam.
Exeunt, marching.

Scene III. [Dunsinane. A room in the Castle.]

Enter *Macbeth, Doctor,* and *Attendants.*

Macb. Bring me no more reports. Let them fly all!
Till Birnam Wood remove to Dunsinane,
I cannot taint with fear. What's the boy Malcolm?
Was he not born of woman? The spirits that know
All mortal consequences have pronounced me thus:
"Fear not, Macbeth. No man that's born of woman
Shall e'er have power upon thee." Then fly, false thanes,
And mingle with the English epicures.
The mind I sway by and the heart I bear
Shall never sag with doubt nor shake with fear.

11. **loon:** stupid rascal.

17. **patch:** fool.

19. **counselors to fear:** i.e., counsel others to fear.

23. **push:** effort.

30. **mouth-honor, breath:** honor on the tongue only, mere words.

31. **fain:** gladly.

Enter *Servant.*

The devil damn thee black, thou cream-faced loon!
Where got'st thou that goose look?
Serv. There is ten thousand—
Macb. Geese, villain?
Serv. Soldiers, sir.
Macb. Go prick thy face and over-red thy fear,
Thou lily-livered boy. What soldiers, patch?
Death of thy soul! Those linen cheeks of thine
Are counselors to fear. What soldiers, whey-face?
Serv. The English force, so please you.
Macb. Take thy face hence.
[*Exit Servant.*]
Seyton!—I am sick at heart,
When I behold—Seyton, I say!—This push
Will cheer me ever, or disseat me now.
I have lived long enough. My way of life
Is fallen into the sere, the yellow leaf;
And that which should accompany old age,
As honor, love, obedience, troops of friends,
I must not look to have; but, in their stead,
Curses not loud but deep, mouth-honor, breath,
Which the poor heart would fain deny, and dare not.
Seyton!

Enter *Seyton.*

Sey. What's your gracious pleasure?
Macb. What news more?

40. **mo:** more; **skirr:** scour.

49. **Raze out:** erase.

50. **oblivious antidote:** medicine producing oblivion.

58-9. **cast/ The water:** that is, make a urinalysis.

60. **pristine:** original.

63. **senna:** a cathartic herb. The First Folio reads "cyme," which can be justified because "cyme" means the outer leaf of the colewort, also a cathartic. The Fourth Folio changed "cyme" to **senna,** and this reading has been generally followed by later editors.

Sey. All is confirmed, my lord, which was reported.
Macb. I'll fight, till from my bones my flesh be hacked.
Give me my armor.
Sey. 'Tis not needed yet.
Macb. I'll put it on.
Send out mo horses, skirr the country round;
Hang those that talk of fear. Give me mine armor.
How does your patient, doctor?
Doct. Not so sick, my lord,
As she is troubled with thick-coming fancies
That keep her from her rest.
Macb. Cure her of that!
Canst thou not minister to a mind diseased,
Pluck from the memory a rooted sorrow,
Raze out the written troubles of the brain,
And with some sweet oblivious antidote
Cleanse the stuffed bosom of that perilous stuff
Which weighs upon the heart?
Doct. Therein the patient
Must minister to himself.
Macb. Throw physic to the dogs, I'll none of it!—
Come, put mine armor on. Give me my staff.
Seyton, send out.—Doctor, the thanes fly from me.—
Come, sir, dispatch.—If thou couldst, doctor, cast
The water of my land, find her disease,
And purge it to a sound and pristine health,
I would applaud thee to the very echo,
That should applaud again.—Pull't off, I say.—
What rhubarb, senna, or what purgative drug,
Would scour these English hence? Hear'st thou of them?

67. **Bring it after me:** i.e., the armor he has taken off.

68. **bane:** destruction.

V. iv. The Scots have met Malcolm and his forces near Birnam Wood, where Malcolm orders each soldier to disguise himself behind a bough. Thus will Birnam Wood move on Dunsinane.

---

2. **chambers will be safe:** i.e., so that we can sleep without fear of being murdered.

7. **shadow:** camouflage.

8. **discovery:** Macbeth's lookouts.

12-3. **endure Our setting down before't:** withstand our siege.

15. **advantage:** opportunity.

Doct. Ay, my good lord. Your royal preparation
Makes us hear something.
Macb. Bring it after me!
I will not be afraid of death and bane
Till Birnam Forest come to Dunsinane.
Doct. [*Aside*] Were I from Dunsinane away and clear,
Profit again should hardly draw me here.
Exeunt.

Scene IV. [Country near Birnam Wood.]

Drum and Colors. Enter *Malcolm, Siward, Macduff, Siward's Son, Menteith, Caithness, Angus,* [*Lennox, Ross,*] and *Soldiers,* marching.

Mal. Cousins, I hope the days are near at hand
That chambers will be safe.
Ment. We doubt it nothing.
Siw. What wood is this before us?
Ment. The wood of Birnam.
Mal. Let every soldier hew him down a bough
And bear't before him. Thereby shall we shadow
The numbers of our host and make discovery
Err in report of us.
Soldiers. It shall be done.
Siw. We learn no other but the confident tyrant
Keeps still in Dunsinane and will endure
Our setting down before't.
Mal. 'Tis his main hope;
For where there is advantage to be given,

16. **more and less:** greater and lesser; classes of all degrees.

17. **constrained things:** men with no will of their own, forced to do as they are told.

18. **too:** that is, as are the persons of their comrades who have deserted.

19-20. **Let our just censures/ Attend the true event:** let us await the outcome before we predict it.

24. **owe:** possess; see I. iv. 11.

26. **certain issue strokes must arbitrate:** the definite outcome must be decided by blows.

27. **Towards which advance the war:** let's proceed with **strokes** toward the **certain issue.**

V. v. Macbeth learns with little show of emotion of his wife's death. A messenger reports that the wood appears to be approaching the castle. For the first time, Macbeth begins to fear that he may have taken false comfort in the prophecies, but he resolves to die in battle.

5. **forced:** reinforced; **those that should be ours:** deserters.

6. **dareful:** defiantly.

Both more and less have given him the revolt;
And none serve with him but constrained things,
Whose hearts are absent too.
Macd. Let our just censures
Attend the true event, and put we on
Industrious soldiership.
Siw. The time approaches
That will with due decision make us know
What we shall say we have, and what we owe.
Thoughts speculative their unsure hopes relate,
But certain issue strokes must arbitrate;
Towards which advance the war.
Exeunt, marching.

Scene V. [Dunsinane. Within the Castle.]

Enter *Macbeth, Seyton,* and *Soldiers,* with *Drum and Colors.*

Macb. Hang out our banners on the outward walls.
The cry is still, "They come!" Our castle's strength
Will laugh a siege to scorn. Here let them lie
Till famine and the ague eat them up.
Were they not forced with those that should be ours,
We might have met them dareful, beard to beard,
And beat them backward home.
A cry within of women.
What is that noise?
Sey. It is the cry of women, my good lord. [*Exit.*]
Macb. I have almost forgot the taste of fears.

12. **fell:** pelt.

13. **dismal treatise:** tale of horror.

15. **Direness:** horror.

16. **start:** stir.

19. **She should have died hereafter:** she should have picked a more convenient time for her death. Macbeth is now so numb from the accumulated horrors of his life that the news of his wife's death has little emotional impact upon him.

The time has been, my senses would have cooled
To hear a night-shriek, and my fell of hair
Would at a dismal treatise rouse and stir
As life were in't. I have supped full with horrors.
Direness, familiar to my slaughterous thoughts,
Cannot once start me.

[Enter *Seyton.*]

Wherefore was that cry?
Sey. The Queen, my lord, is dead.
Macb. She should have died hereafter;
There would have been a time for such a word.
Tomorrow, and tomorrow, and tomorrow
Creeps in this petty pace from day to day
To the last syllable of recorded time;
And all our yesterdays have lighted fools
The way to dusty death. Out, out, brief candle!
Life's but a walking shadow, a poor player,
That struts and frets his hour upon the stage
And then is heard no more. It is a tale
Told by an idiot, full of sound and fury,
Signifying nothing.

Enter a *Messenger.*

Thou com'st to use thy tongue. Thy story quickly!
Mess. Gracious my lord,
I should report that which I say I saw,
But know not how to do't.
Macb. Well, say, sir!

45. **cling:** wither; **sooth:** truth; see I. ii. 40.

47. **pull:** rein. Macbeth's courage is shaken and his resolution falters.

48. **doubt:** fear; **equivocation of the fiend:** trickery of the devil's agents; see **equivocator,** II. iii. 8.

52. **avouches:** affirms.

56. **wrack:** wreck, ruin; see I. iii. 123.

57. **harness:** armor.

V. vi. Malcolm and his forces reach the castle and throw down their boughs.

Macbeth on the battlefield.

From Olaus Magnus, *Historia de gentibus septentrionalibus* (1555).

Mess. As I did stand my watch upon the hill,
I looked toward Birnam, and anon methought
The wood began to move.

Macb. Liar and slave!

Mess. Let me endure your wrath if't be not so.
Within this three mile may you see it coming;
I say, a moving grove.

Macb. If thou speak'st false,
Upon the next tree shalt thou hang alive,
Till famine cling thee. If thy speech be sooth,
I care not if thou dost for me as much.
I pull in resolution, and begin
To doubt the equivocation of the fiend,
That lies like truth. "Fear not, till Birnam Wood
Do come to Dunsinane!" and now a wood
Comes toward Dunsinane. Arm, arm, and out!
If this which he avouches does appear,
There is nor flying hence nor tarrying here.
I 'gin to be aweary of the sun,
And wish the estate o' the world were now undone.
Ring the alarum bell! Blow wind, come wrack,
At least we'll die with harness on our back!

Exeunt.

Scene VI. [Dunsinane. Before the Castle.]

Drum and Colors. Enter *Malcolm, Siward, Macduff,* and their *Army,* with boughs.

Mal. Now near enough. Your leavy screens throw down

3. **show like those you are:** appear like yourselves.

5. **battle:** battleline.

7. **order:** plan of battle.

9. **power:** forces.

13. **harbingers:** forerunners, announcers; see I. iv. 51.

V. vii. Macbeth has left the safety of the castle to fight in the open field. He kills young Siward, son of the Earl of Northumberland. When he has moved off, Macduff appears seeking him. The castle has surrendered with little resistance and many of Macbeth's own men have joined his enemies.

1-2. **They have tied me to a stake. I cannot fly/ But bearlike I must fight the course:** in the popular sport of bearbaiting, the bear was tied to a stake while dogs attacked him.

And show like those you are. You, worthy uncle,
Shall with my cousin, your right noble son,
Lead our first battle. Worthy Macduff and we
Shall take upon's what else remains to do,
According to our order.
Siw. Fare you well.
Do we but find the tyrant's power tonight,
Let us be beaten if we cannot fight.
Macd. Make all our trumpets speak, give them all breath,
Those clamorous harbingers of blood and death.
Exeunt. Alarums continued.

Scene VII. [Another part of the field.]

Enter *Macbeth.*

Macb. They have tied me to a stake. I cannot fly,
But bearlike I must fight the course. What's he
That was not born of woman? Such a one
Am I to fear, or none.

Enter *Young Siward.*

Y. Siw. What is thy name?
Macb. Thou'lt be afraid to hear it.
Y. Siw. No; though thou call'st thyself a hotter name
Than any is in hell.
Macb. My name's Macbeth.

22. **staves:** spears.

24. **undeeded:** unused; having performed no deed of valor.

26. **bruited:** reported.

28. **gently rendered:** surrendered with little or no resistance.

31. **itself professes:** announces itself.

An Irish kern with his stave.

From an 1883 reprint of John Derricke, *The Image of Ireland* (1581).

Y. Siw. The devil himself could not pronounce a title
More hateful to mine ear.

Macb. No, nor more fearful.

Y. Siw. Thou liest, abhorred tyrant! With my sword
I'll prove the lie thou speak'st.

Fight, and Young Siward slain.

Macb. Thou wast born of woman.
But swords I smile at, weapons laugh to scorn,
Brandished by man that's of a woman born. *Exit.*

Alarums. Enter *Macduff.*

Macd. That way the noise is. Tyrant, show thy face!
If thou beest slain and with no stroke of mine,
My wife and children's ghosts will haunt me still.
I cannot strike at wretched kerns, whose arms
Are hired to bear their staves. Either thou, Macbeth,
Or else my sword with an unbattered edge
I sheathe again undeeded. There thou shouldst be.
By this great clatter one of greatest note
Seems bruited. Let me find him, Fortune!
And more I beg not. *Exit. Alarums.*

Enter *Malcolm* and *Siward.*

Siw. This way, my lord. The castle's gently rendered:
The tyrant's people on both sides do fight;
The noble thanes do bravely in the war;
The day almost itself professes yours,
And little is to do.

V. viii. Macduff finds Macbeth, who is reluctant to fight because he has enough of the blood of Macduff's kin on his head and feels certain he will win. When Macduff tells him that he was prematurely ripped from his mother's womb, therefore not a man born of woman, Macbeth recoils in fear. Rather than be captured alive and be treated as a spectacle, he engages with Macduff, who cuts off his head and announces Scotland's freedom from tyranny.

2. **lives:** living enemies.

10. **give thee out:** report thee.

12. **intrenchant:** invulnerable; unable to be trenched (gashed).

Mal. We have met with foes
That strike beside us.
Siw. Enter, sir, the castle.
Exeunt. Alarum.

Scene VIII. [Another part of the field.]

Enter *Macbeth.*

Macb. Why should I play the Roman fool and die
On mine own sword? Whiles I see lives, the gashes
Do better upon them.

Enter *Macduff.*

Macd. Turn, hellhound, turn!
Macb. Of all men else I have avoided thee.
But get thee back! My soul is too much charged
With blood of thine already.
Macd. I have no words;
My voice is in my sword, thou bloodier villain
Than terms can give thee out!
Fight. Alarum.
Macb. Thou losest labor.
As easy mayst thou the intrenchant air
With thy keen sword impress as make me bleed.
Let fall thy blade on vulnerable crests.
I bear a charmed life, which must not yield
To one of woman born.
Macd. Despair thy charm!

24. **palter:** double-deal, equivocate.

30. **Painted upon a pole:** that is, his likeness painted and set on a pole to advertise the display of his person, as in a sideshow. The Elizabethans were fond of curiosities such as are still displayed at fairs and circuses.

S.D. after l. 39. The Stage Direction in the First Folio contains the additional line "Enter Fighting, and Macbeth slaine." Previous editors have noted that prompt copies marked for varying occasions sometimes have conflicting or duplicating stage directions. This may be an example.

41. **go off:** die.

42. **cheaply bought:** that is, few of their men have been killed.

And let the angel whom thou still hast served
Tell thee, Macduff was from his mother's womb
Untimely ripped.

Macb. Accursed be that tongue that tells me so,
For it hath cowed my better part of man!
And be these juggling fiends no more believed,
That palter with us in a double sense,
That keep the word of promise to our ear
And break it to our hope! I'll not fight with thee!

Macd. Then yield thee, coward,
And live to be the show and gaze o' the time!
We'll have thee, as our rarer monsters are,
Painted upon a pole, and underwrit
"Here may you see the tyrant."

Macb. I will not yield,
To kiss the ground before young Malcolm's feet
And to be baited with the rabble's curse.
Though Birnam Wood be come to Dunsinane,
And thou opposed, being of no woman born,
Yet I will try the last. Before my body
I throw my warlike shield. Lay on, Macduff,
And damned be him that first cries "Hold, enough!"

Exeunt fighting. Alarums.

Retreat and flourish. Enter, with *Drum and Colors, Malcolm, Siward, Ross, Thanes,* and *Soldiers.*

Mal. I would the friends we miss were safe arrived.

Siw. Some must go off; and yet, by these I see,
So great a day as this is cheaply bought.

Mal. Macduff is missing, and your noble son.

47. **unshrinking station where he fought:** i.e., the spot where he held his ground and fought it out.

62. **parted:** departed.

65. **The time is free:** our country is freed from tyranny.

66. **compassed:** surrounded; **thy kingdom's pearl:** the chief ornaments of Scotland, its noblest men.

The victors with the heads of the vanquished.

From an 1883 reprint of John Derricke, *The Image of Ireland* (1581).

Ross. Your son, my lord, has paid a soldier's debt.
He only lived but till he was a man,
The which no sooner had his prowess confirmed
In the unshrinking station where he fought
But like a man he died.
Siw. Then he is dead?
Ross. Ay, and brought off the field. Your cause of sorrow
Must not be measured by his worth, for then
It hath no end.
Siw. Had he his hurts before?
Ross. Ay, on the front.
Siw. Why then, God's soldier be he!
Had I as many sons as I have hairs,
I would not wish them to a fairer death.
And so his knell is knolled.
Mal. He's worth more sorrow,
And that I'll spend for him.
Siw. He's worth no more.
They say he parted well and paid his score,
And so, God be with him! Here comes newer comfort.

Enter *Macduff*, with *Macbeth's* head.

Macd. Hail, King! for so thou art. Behold where stands
The usurper's cursed head. The time is free.
I see thee compassed with thy kingdom's pearl,
That speak my salutation in their minds;
Whose voices I desire aloud with mine—
Hail, King of Scotland!
All. Hail, King of Scotland! *Flourish.*
Mal. We shall not spend a large expense of time

72-3. **reckon with your several loves/ And make us even with you:** calculate the devotion each of you has shown and repay you.

76. **would be planted newly with the time:** should be done among our first reforms.

79. **Producing forth:** haling forth from hiding.

81. **self and violent hands:** her own violent hands.

83. **Grace:** i.e., Divine Grace.

Before we reckon with your several loves
And make us even with you. My Thanes and kinsmen,
Henceforth be Earls, the first that ever Scotland
In such an honor named. What's more to do
Which would be planted newly with the time–
As calling home our exiled friends abroad
That fled the snares of watchful tyranny,
Producing forth the cruel ministers
Of this dead butcher and his fiendlike queen,
Who (as 'tis thought) by self and violent hands
Took off her life–this, and what needful else
That calls upon us, by the grace of Grace
We will perform in measure, time, and place.
So thanks to all at once and to each one,
Whom we invite to see us crowned at Scone.

Flourish. Exeunt omnes.

KEY TO

Famous Lines and Phrases

Fair is foul, and foul is fair. [*Witches*–I. i. 12]

So foul and fair a day I have not seen. [*Macbeth*–I. iii. 39]

Nothing in his life
Became him like the leaving it. [*Malcolm*–I. iv. 8-9]

Yet do I fear thy nature.
It is too full o' the milk of human kindness . . .
[*Lady Macbeth*–I. v. 15-6]

Come, you spirits
That tend on mortal thoughts, unsex me here . . .
[*Lady Macbeth*–I. v. 44-5]

. . . look like the innocent flower,
But be the serpent under't. [*Lady Macbeth*–I. v. 73-4]

If it were done when 'tis done, then 'twere well
It were done quickly . . . [*Macbeth*–I. vii. 1-2]

Is this a dagger which I see before me,
The handle toward my hand? . . . [*Macbeth*–II. i. 42-3]

Sleep that knits up the raveled sleave of care . . .
[*Macbeth*–II. ii. 51]

Will all great Neptune's ocean wash this blood
Clean from my hand? . . . [*Macbeth*–II. ii. 78-9]

Naught's had, all's spent,
Where our desire is got without content.
[*Lady Macbeth*–III. ii. 6-7]

We have scotched the snake, not killed it.
[*Macbeth*–III. ii. 15]

Duncan is in his grave;
After life's fitful fever he sleeps well.
[*Macbeth*–III. ii. 24-5]

. . . I am cabined, cribbed, confined, bound in
To saucy doubts and fears. [*Macbeth*–III. iv. 30-1]

It will have blood, they say: blood will have blood.
[*Macbeth*–III. iv. 152-53]

Double, double, toil and trouble;
Fire burn, and cauldron bubble. [*Witches*–IV. i. 10-1]

. . . I'll make assurance double sure . . .
[*Macbeth*–IV. i. 93]

Angels are bright still, though the brightest fell.
[*Malcolm*–IV. iii. 25]

At one fell swoop . . . [*Macduff*–IV. iii. 256]

Out, damned spot! out, I say! [*Lady Macbeth*–V. i. 31]

All the perfumes of Arabia will not sweeten
this little hand. [*Lady Macbeth*–V. i. 46-7]

What's done cannot be undone. [*Lady Macbeth*–V. i. 62-3]

I have lived long enough. My way of life
Is fallen into the sere, the yellow leaf . . .
[*Macbeth*–V. iii. 25-6]

Canst thou not minister to a mind diseased . . .
[*Macbeth*–V. iii. 47]

I have supped full with horrors. [*Macbeth*–V. v. 14]

Tomorrow, and tomorrow, and tomorrow . . .
[*Macbeth*–V. v. 21]

I 'gin to be aweary of the sun . . . [*Macbeth*–V. v. 54]

. . . Lay on, Macduff,
And damned be him that first cries "Hold, enough!"
[*Macbeth*–V. viii. 38-9]